The Norwich School

The Crafts (textile)
Department

INDIGO
MADDER
&
MARIGOLD

INDIGO
MADDER
&
MARIGOLD

A PORTFOLIO
OF COLORS FROM
NATURAL DYES

TRUDY VAN STRALEN

INDIGO, MADDER & MARIGOLD
A Portfolio of Colors from Natural Dyes

by Trudy Van Stralen

Design/Susan Strawn
Production/Marc M. Owens
Photography/Rick Mastelli and Joe Coca

Text © 1993, Trudy Van Stralen
Photography on pages 10–59 © 1993, Rick Mastelli, and on the cover and pages 60–124 © 1993, Joe Coca and Interweave Press, Inc.

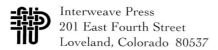 Interweave Press
201 East Fourth Street
Loveland, Colorado 80537

Library of Congress Cataloging-in-Publication Data

Van Stralen, Trudy, 1942–
     Indigo, madder & marigold : a portfolio of colors from natural
dyes / Trudy van Stralen.
          p.   cm.
     Includes bibliographical references and index.
     ISBN 0-934026-86-6 : $29.95
     1. Dyes and dyeing, Domestic. 2. Dyes and dyeing--Textile
fibers. 3. Dye plants. I. Title
TT854.3.V36   1993
667'.3--dc20
                                              9328718
                                              CIP

First printing: 993:15M:CC

Printed in Hong Kong by Sing Cheong

*To the memory
of my son, Wouter,
who gave me
the inspiration to
persevere with the
writing of this book.*

ACKNOWLEDGEMENTS

I would like to thank my editors and publisher, especially Betsy Strauch, Jane Patrick, and Rita Buchanan. I do not know whether they really understood what they were in for when Linda Ligon talked me into writing this book. Their patience and extra help were essential in overcoming my use of English as a second language.

I would also like to thank master spinners Stephenie Gaustad, for her handspun cotton, and Patricia Emerick, for many skeins of handspun silk and other exotic fibers. Also thanks to Heddy King, of On the Inca Trail, who supplied me with skeins of alpaca yarn.

Finally, I would like to thank those I shared our house with during the writing of this book. My husband, Jan, daughter, Judy, and my mother. They lived through my ups and downs, prepared the dye facilities, helped with the samples, and more. They were part of the process, concept to proofreading the manuscript. Without their support and continued encouragement I would not have been able to complete this work.

Trudy Van Stralen
Prescott, Ontario

C O N T E N T S

P R E F A C E

ANCIENT FABRICS whose colors are still rich and vibrant abound in museums and private collections. Peruvian burial cloths that date back more than 2000 years, Coptic tapestries from fifth-century Egypt, Han Dynasty carpets from China, and fourteenth-century Medieval tapestries all used a full spectrum of hues. It was not unusual for these fabrics to incorporate dozens, or even hundreds, of carefully controlled shades of purple, red, blue, green, brown, black, and gold. No color was beyond the reach of our ancient forebears. But the craft of producing natural colors largely disappeared after the 1850s, when chemical dyes began to provide a cheap and easy alternative.

Somehow, when natural dyes became of interest again after the middle of this century, the emphasis was on using local wild plants, most of which yield colors in the yellow-to-tan range. The pleasure of using materials at hand superseded the desire for vivid, varied hues.

Yet the dyestuffs of antiquity have remained available, and methods for using them to produce the richest, fastest, most fully nuanced colors have been revived. Deriving color from renewable resources rather than from petroleum has become a serious concern, and nature provides a way. With this book, natural dyeing comes full circle.

Linda Ligon

Spinning, dyeing, and weaving are part of the natural rhythm
of life at my family's eastern Ontario farm.

INTRODUCTION

SINCE I ARRIVED in Canada more than twenty-six years ago, my long-standing interest in fibers has drawn me in many directions. One of them led to experiments with color and dyeing and, eventually, this book.

When we—my husband, Jan, our son, Wouter, and I—moved from Holland to our new country, our dream was to live on a farm someday. After years of searching the countryside (by which time our family numbered four children), we found our farm, north of Prescott in eastern Ontario. There was a 186-year-old 25-by-25-foot log house (well kept but with no indoor plumbing); but more important, especially to Wouter and myself,

was the land, 150 acres which had not been farmed for fifteen years. It was all small pastures with old cedar fences and stone piles, trees and shrubs, and lots of lichens on rocks and trees. A neighboring farmer called it artistic country but unsuitable for farming.

We explored the property and found deer and rabbit prints in the snow. We persuaded Jan not to listen to our farmer friend. All he really needed was a large plot of good soil for a vegetable garden, having outgrown the backyard garden in the village where we were then living. Wouter kept rabbits in the town garage, not one or two but "many", and needed larger quarters, too. If you're thinking,

Rugged fields and woods make farming a challenge, but yield
both color inspiration and abundant native dyestuffs.

Here is my husband, Jan, with a few of the many
sheep which have provided wool for my dyepots
and manure for the garden.

"These people didn't know anything about farming," you're right! We grew up in the city, and all our farm knowledge was out of books. But in April 1974, we took the big step and moved to the farm. It was cold and muddy, and our bathroom facilities were outside. Wouter had just turned eight, David was not quite six, Claudia, three, and Judy, not yet a year old.

Jan went to work, and I stayed home to look after the kids and the creatures. Farm animals arrived before the indoor plumbing. One day, Jan came home with two sheep, mother and son, because he wanted their manure to improve the garden soil. For lack of good fencing, we tethered them outside. My city upbringing gave me some warped ideas about farming. For example, when it rained, I first went to fetch the "poor" tethered animals and put them in the barn, then ran to bring in the laundry (we didn't have sufficient electrical power to run a dryer), and finally took my wet baby out of the playpen. I'll tell you, I was quite slim in those days. A neighbor pointed out that if the animals were loose in the pasture, they would not be going in the barn when it rained. Well, one learns!

My Dutch upbringing to "waste not, want not" and my interest in fibers made me go into spinning. I felt we had to do something with the good wool the sheep were producing (it was actually not very good, being full of kemp and very short). About this time, Jan's uncle came for a visit. He had learned to spin wool during the Second World War. I bought a locally made Saxony wheel, and he taught me the basics of spinning, but the wheel was so fast that the yarn came out hard and overtwisted. Even though it was very itchy, I used that yarn to knit a hat for Wouter. He was overjoyed and wore it without complaining.

I often use different colored wools as well as white in the same dyepot for different shades that go together well.

My experience with fiber dates back to my schooldays, when everyone learned to knit, crochet, and sew. I was taught well, and enjoyed working with yarn and fabric. Over the years, I took several courses in fashion design and pattern making. I sewed and embroidered my wedding dress, and sewed all the family's clothes for many years. The only problem was getting good fabric. It was almost impossible to find nice woolens, so along with learning to spin, I decided to learn to weave my own cloth.

The local college offered a course in frame weaving, and the teacher also knew a bit about spinning, so I enrolled. That's where I was introduced to natural dyeing. Later, I took more courses at the college as well as one from Nell Znamierowski, who inspired me to "play" with colors. I decided to start a business, Hilltop Wools, and soon had a store filled with fluffy, brightly dyed fleeces, dyed handspun yarns, and spinning, weaving, and dyeing supplies.

When I get into something, I always put forth every effort to make it a success. When I began to spin, I made it a full-time job and spun a minimum of eight hours a day. After a year, I felt I knew something about spinning and had mastered some of the techniques, but I found just plain spinning somewhat boring. I liked it best when I was spinning and designing yarn with different colors. Dyeing turned out to be my favorite part of the whole business.

The colors that come from the dyepots are so beautiful to look at
that I'm almost sorry to use them.

16

The colors I see walking around the farm always inspire me to try
new combinations in my dyeing, spinning, and weaving.

THE COLORS OF NATURE

Our farm is surrounded by rough country with lots of wildflowers and trees. Every year, the parade of colors is repeated: along with the great variety of greens come the soft pink blossoms in early spring, the bold reds and yellows in summer, the vibrant reds, oranges, yellows, and rusts in fall, and the grays, browns, and evergreen hues of winter with its beautiful cochineal/indigo sunsets. Every year, I wish I could create all these colors with dyestuffs. Though I never get to all of them, I feel that many colors in nature can be matched with natural dyes.

I started trying to duplicate nature's colors by following recipes in books. Jan

Even though I work mostly with purchased dyestuffs,
I always plant a generous amount of marigolds,
coreopsis, and other dyeplants in the garden.

gave me my first book on natural dyes. When my mother-in-law saw it, she said, "More work!" Farm life was already hard work, especially in the summer with its long days and very short nights to rest up, but I was intrigued and spent many hours experimenting.

I discovered that many recipes were the same in different books, and many did not work even though I followed the directions carefully. Too frequently, the colors were drab, and I hate drab colors. Furthermore, the dyed wool often felt harsh. Experienced spinners told me that dyeing loose fleece would cause it to mat so I should spin it first, then wash out the grease very well. They advised using large amounts of mordants to make the dye fast, then adding just a bit of dyestuff—as in the books. I followed their advice; however, one recipe called for a half cup of tin mordant per pound of wool, and the wool completely disintegrated! These early experiments raised many questions.

I had no training in chemistry. I knew that doing this or that would cause a certain chemical reaction, but I didn't know why. When I took my questions to my children's high school science teachers and to chemical engineer friends, they told me I should take a chemistry course, but the information I needed was too specific to obtain even from several courses. I've learned most of my dye strategies by experience.

The whole family became involved. Our outings into the woods now had a purpose: to collect dyestuffs. We explored the farm and found all kinds of materials to try; if they resulted in nice colors, we collected more.

We went farther afield. One Canadian Thanksgiving weekend, we visited friends who had half a dozen walnut trees. We picked up every single walnut—eight feed bags full—from their yard. This gave me plenty of dyestuff, but then neighbors began calling to see

I love the carpets of lilies of the valley that bloom in early spring.
And they make lovely, soft greens in the dyepot.

whether I would like more walnuts or different kinds of sawdust, and so forth.

One Saturday in November when Judy was three, all four children went out and didn't come home for hours. I was concerned, but Jan was in on the plot. That night, I questioned the kids as I tried to scrub the orange stains from their hands, but nobody would say anything. The next day, my birthday, they presented me with a large shopping bag of lichens they had scraped off the rocks (Wouter had taught them not to take all the lichens from one spot). It was one of the nicest presents I've ever received.

Using local dye plants gave me a limited range of colors, with no blues or reds. Gradually, I started experimenting with cochineal, madder, sandalwood, and other purchased dyes. Used alone or mixed with the local dyes, these greatly extended my color range and sometimes increased the fastness of the colors.

I experimented with indigo, again with the family's help. Indigo dye as purchased is insoluble in water. Vat dyeing requires a reducing agent to make the indigo dissolve, but this also changes it into a colorless form. When the dyed fiber is exposed to the air, the dye is oxidized and changed back to the familiar dark blue color. The traditional reducing agent is stale urine, preferably from young boys. . . . I tried this technique but didn't like it very much. At about the same time, I tried a recipe for Saxon blue, in which powdered indigo is dissolved in sulfuric acid; then the resulting solution is added dropwise to the dyepot. I found this form much more convenient to apply and mix with other dyes.

19

I started asking questions and researching their answers. Could I find a way to dye wool in the fleece? By now, we had at least twenty fleeces, and I couldn't spin them all into yarn in one winter. Besides, it would far more interesting spinning dyed fleeces than white ones. I was doing my dyeing in summer outdoors on stone fireplaces. We had started with small kettles, but when we realized what

Two large dyepots—one with Saxon blue and one with cochineal—
will give a good range of blues, reds, pinks, and purples.

large quantities we would be processing for my business, Jan built larger fireplaces and we bought four huge stainless steel kettles. The largest can easily hold ten full feed bags of walnuts.

I found that I could dye twenty-five to fifty pounds of fleece at once over the wood fire without its matting. To avoid extra handling, I used only one-pot dyebaths. It gave me great pleasure in the af-

ternoon to see great piles of fluffy fleece in different shades lying on sheets in the yard. The kids helped tease the fleece apart to dry and learned that a "good" job meant not to expose any of the sheet beneath the wool. This was tedious!

I wouldn't dye if rain was forecast but if a storm did come up suddenly, all the family would run outside, roll up the sheets covered with fleece, and carry

Even the common field weeds offer up soft yellows, golds, and tans in the dyepot.

them inside. We normally spread the fleece to dry in the hot sun. I felt that if a color couldn't stand that treatment, it wouldn't stay in at all. Sometimes a color did fade, usually because the bath hadn't been hot enough or mordanting had been inadequate. In either case, I just dyed the fleece again.

I wondered what would happen if I washed the fleece with a milder cleaning product. Would the remaining grease resist the dyestuffs? Books said that you need strong detergent to get rid of the natural grease. I achieved my goal of obtaining brightly colored fleeces with

some variations in color mainly by leaving some of the grease in. The grease worked as a resist on the locks: the tips were much darker with a lovely shading toward the cut ends.

Would the colors still be fast if I used less mordant? I started using a fraction of the mordants called for in most books. I found that temperatures needed to be rather hot for colorfastness. For a couple of years, I made samples of the dyed fiber and tested them for lightfastness in a south window for a year. Then I had some sample blankets woven and tested them for washfastness. The colors made with reduced amounts of mordants seem to stand up remarkably well.

If I started with more dyestuff in the pot, could I use this bath for more than one batch of fiber? I suspected that our ancestors would have used small amounts of mordants together with larger quantities of dyestuffs. When I tried this, I found that I could indeed use a single dyebath for successive batches.

Many people who saw my colors commented, "Nice colors, but you must have been lucky," and, "You'll never get that color again; that is the way with natural dyes." Here was a new challenge. I developed a system of recipes based on percentages, by which I can get similar colors time after time. I use a metric scale like that used in laboratories around the world to weigh out my fibers, mordants, and dyestuffs. Weighing in grams is much more accurate than measuring by teaspoons, tablespoons, and cups, and it's easy to calculate percentages with metric measurement. My colors are now so close that I can't see the difference from one dyebath to the next, unless, for example, I've used flowers picked at different stages in the two baths.

Another technique I have developed is mixing natural dyestuffs, just as other dyers mix synthetic dyes. I often combine two dyes, such as cochineal and walnut, in the same dyepot to obtain a wider range of colors.

Colors dyed during the short Canadian summer give me plenty of color for knitting and weaving thoughout the winter.

ABOUT THIS BOOK

I wrote this book to share my techniques and recipes for making beautiful colors the natural way. First, I'll show you how to measure ingredients accurately—the key to successful natural dyeing. Then I'll explain how to use mordants safely and effectively, and tell how to prepare and handle wool, mohair, silk, cotton and other natural fibers. One chapter gives step-by-step directions for making many colors from just a few pots, just as we do in the three-day workshops that I teach. Finally, there are descriptions of all my favorite dyestuffs, with recipes, directions, and photos of the gorgeous colors they can produce.

Careful measuring is the key to predictable and repeatable colors. Here, I'm adding cochineal, thoroughly ground up and accurately weighed, to 200 ml of water.

Equipment & How to Use It

Always use a separate set of equipment for dyeing. Never use a tool for cooking if it has ever been used for dyeing.

Work site

Find a safe place to do your dyeing. You should rule out the kitchen as a potential studio right away. Though not all dyebaths are poisonous, some are, and it is too easy to reach for a snack or put supper on to cook while you are in the middle of a dyeing session. I started out doing all my dyeing outdoors. Now I have a studio where I can dye indoors in winter, but in summer I still prefer to do my dyeing outdoors. Good ventilation is important, so choose a site that is as open as possible: a garage with the door open, for instance, is airy but also sheltered from the rain.

Heat source

I have always used a wood stove for heating my dyepots, but that's because I have lots of wood on hand. I've learned by trial and error which is the right wood for quick fires or for those that have to last longer.

I've used many kinds of camp stoves at my workshops and find that the two-burner propane stoves are easiest to work with. I have struggled with traditional camp stoves that run on liquid fuel, but they are fine if you have one and can make it work.

If you decide to use an electric hot plate, you'll need a heavy-duty extension cord placed so that you don't trip over it or the stove with a full pot of dyestuff. A sturdy picnic table comes in handy to set a stove on. If you're concerned about stains, cover the table with plastic, but don't place a hot pot directly on the plastic. Instead, use a fire-resistant hotpad.

No matter what kind of stove you choose, keep a fire extinguisher nearby and know how to use it.

Water

I use our well water for dyeing. It's very pure and almost neutral, neither acid nor alkaline. You can use tap water, rain water, or whatever is available. I've taught dye workshops in many places, and sometimes the water was so rich in minerals that it stained the bathroom fixtures, but surprisingly, the colors turned out all right anyway. Where there was a lot of iron in the water, the colors were slightly grayed and not as clear, but they turned out better than I would have expected. Perhaps water quality is less important with the concentrated dyebaths I use than it might be with weaker dyebaths.

I do my dyeing outdoors in large stainless steel vats over wood heat. For smaller quantities, you can use canning kettles and camp stoves.

DYEPOTS

The size pot to use depends on the amount of fiber you would like to dye at one time. If you plan to dye only a few small skeins of yarn, a one-gallon pot will do. For fleece or yardage, it's better to use a five-gallon or larger pot. The pot should be large enough that the material to be dyed can move around easily in the dye liquid and the liquid level is not so high that it bubbles over when it comes to the boil.

The best dyepots are made of stainless steel. They don't react with the dyestuff or influence the color, and you can scrub them completely clean after each use. A restaurant supply store is a good source of stainless steel pots, and secondhand stores in rural areas sometimes have stainless steel milk kettles, the kind used before central milking systems were in-

stalled on dairy farms. Look for thick, heavy pots, even though they cost more, because dyes will stick and burn onto cheap, lightweight pots.

Enamel pots are less expensive than stainless steel, but they chip easily, exposing the iron beneath, which reacts with the dyestuff and can stain or spot the fiber. Pyrex pots are nonreactive, but most are too small to dye anything but samples. It's possible to use aluminum, copper, or iron pots, but these metals react with the dyes and influence the color, sometimes in unpredictable or undesirable ways.

PAILS

Plastic pails of various sizes are handy for soaking fiber and dyestuff in, receiving strained dye liquid, and holding other liquids that don't need to be simmered, such as ammonia afterbath. Restaurants receive many of their supplies in plastic pails, which they usually throw away when empty; they may be willing to give you some.

STIRRING STICKS

I prefer smooth wooden dowels about 1/2 inch thick for stirring my dyebaths. Three are enough. You'll need a glass stirring rod for preparing the Saxon blue indigo solution.

PROTECTIVE CLOTHING

A pair of rubber gloves is essential. For most dyeing activities, old clothes will be fine. In summer when I'm working outside, I just wear shorts and a T-shirt; they do get dirty, or nicely colored! Otherwise, I usually wear a lab coat. I recommend wearing a dust mask when grinding cochineal or crushing dried plants.

EQUIPMENT TO GRIND AND REDUCE DYESTUFF

The finer the pieces of dyestuff, the more color that can be extracted from them. I use pruning shears to cut branches and roots into small pieces. A mortar and pestle can be used to grind small quantities of dyestuff, but an electric coffee grinder is faster and more efficient. I use one to grind cochineal insects to a powder. They're about $20 new. Look for a used one at garage sales.

DYE EXTRACTOR

When I'm dyeing small quantities, I spin the excess dye liquid out of my fiber with a salad spinner. For larger quantities, I use the spinner from an old washing machine. I return the extracted liquid, which is still warm, to the dyepot and continue with another run. (This is especially important with the concentrated dyebaths that I make. I don't want to waste any dye, nor let the fluid in the dyepot get too low.) The extractor is also good for spinning out rinse water and minimizes the handling of delicate fleeces.

THERMOMETER

Some dyes need to be heated to a certain temperature to ensure colorfastness, particularly lightfastness; others must not be allowed to boil; and fiber should never boil. Like weighing dyestuffs accurately, measuring the temperature carefully helps to ensure repeatability of a given color. A candy thermometer will do the job, and you can clip it on the edge of the dyepot. An immersible laboratory thermometer from a scientific supply company will cost a little more but is more accurate.

Here, I'm adding yarn which has been dyed with cochineal to the saxon blue pot for a nice purple.

STRAINING EQUIPMENT

When brewing tea, you can either use a tea bag (or tea ball) or brew loose tea and strain out the tea leaves. It's the same with separating flowers, nuts, roots, and branches after they've been simmered in water to extract their dye. I sometimes stuff the dyestuff *loosely* into old pantyhose, making sure that water can circulate freely through the particles so that they will yield as much color as possible. To hold a large batch of dyestuff, I sew a piece of old sheet into a bag. If I have simmered the dyestuff without first putting it in a bag or pantyhose, I'll strain the dye liquid through a stainless steel milk strainer lined with a piece of old sheet. The advantage to this method is that the bits of dyestuff can circulate more thoroughly in the dyepot than they can in a bag. The disadvantage is that the hot liquid in a large kettle may be awkward to pour without spilling. You could let it cool first, but waiting wastes valuable time.

METRIC SCALE

My dye recipes are repeatable because I take accurate measurements—by weight, not by volume. The system of teaspoons, tablespoons, and cups works fine in baking but not so well in dyeing. Such measurements can easily be off by 10 percent or more. Measuring by weight in grams is much more accurate, and using the metric system makes it very easy to do calculations.

A metric scale is a very important tool for dyeing. Because you'll be measuring very small quantities of mordants, it should be accurate to 0.1 gram (1/10 of one gram). Metric scales are readily available from scientific or laboratory supply companies (check the Yellow Pages). They cost about $100 or more. One of my students told me she got a good buy on one at a police auction. That's right—it was a drug scale!

The scale you buy will probably come with its own instructions, but the principle of weighing will be the same for any scale. You first need to calibrate it, that is, adjust the zero point. Next, weigh a container—paper bag, margarine tub, or whatever—that will hold what you're weighing. Add that weight to the weight of fiber, mordant, or dyestuff you need, and set the scale for the total weight. Now, gradually fill the container until the scale balances (or otherwise indicates that the total weight has been obtained).

OTHER MEASURING EQUIPMENT

Other measuring equipment can be scavenged. You'll need a few plastic spoons for scooping powdered dyestuffs and mordants out of containers. Save some margarine tubs for weighing mordants or dyes and mixing them with hot water. You can use paper or plastic grocery bags to hold yarn, fleece, or bulky dyestuffs for weighing.

KEEPING RECORDS

Keep a notebook handy and always write down what fiber, dyestuff, and mordant you're using, how much everything weighs, and how you proceed with the dyeing. Then attach samples of the dyed fiber or yarn. Keeping records helps you learn from your experiments and makes it possible to follow the same steps to repeat a given color anytime you want.

WHY USE METRIC WEIGHTS?

The metric system of measuring weight in grams and kilograms is much more straightforward than the English system of pounds and ounces because it involves no awkward fractions. Metric units are especially convenient when you use recipes like mine, which are based on percentages of the weight of the fiber. Here is an example:

Weigh 100 grams (g) of fiber. 100 g = 3.5 oz.

For mordanting, use 10% of that weight in alum: .10 x 100 g = 10 g alum. (.10 x 3.5 oz = 0.35 oz.)

For dyeing, use 50% of the weight of the fiber in dyestuff: .50 x 100 g = 50 g dyestuff. (.50 x 3.5 oz = 1.75 oz.)

You can see that the calculations are a breeze in the metric system, but extremely cumbersome in English units. Further, it's next to impossible to weigh out 0.35 ounces or 1.75 ounces on a scale graduated in ounces.

You can keep using a cochineal dyepot until every bit of color is gone. Even the palest pinks are lovely, and fun to mix with the slightly darker shades.

PREPARATIONS FOR DYEING

Natural dyes can be used to color wool, mohair, silk, flax, cotton, and other natural fibers, and can be applied to unspun fibers, to yarn, and to fabric. Whatever material you choose, a few simple steps will prepare it for dyeing. These include washing and weighing, which are described in this chapter. Many dye processes also require mordanting, which is described in the next chapter.

CHOOSING FIBER

Fibers vary in their affinity for dyes. Wools—especially medium-coarse and coarse wool—are easy to handle and dye readily. Fine wools require more care in handling and may not dye as dark. Mohair dyes easily and has a pretty luster. Silk dyes well if it is properly mordanted. Plant fibers such as cotton and flax are more difficult to dye with the dyes I like to use, and require extra time and more steps to produce intense hues. Plant materials used for basketry can be dyed, but they are not discussed in this book, and neither are synthetic fibers.

PREPARING WOOL OR MOHAIR FLEECE FOR DYEING

White wool is an obvious candidate for dyeing, but naturally colored fleeces can also be dyed with natural dyes. Light gray fleeces often have some white fibers which take up more color than the gray fibers do. The result is a rich, warm, heathery look that spinners love.

Always use your best fleece. Some people dye their leftovers, thinking to improve their appearance, but this is never success-ful. If the fleece is dirty or matted to start with, it will only look worse when dyed.

If fleece is not too fine, is fairly clean, and is to be dyed in medium and dark colors, you can leave it unwashed. The grease, which tends to be distributed unevenly along the locks, works as a resist, giving a lovely shading that is especially effective on mohair and long wools, and fun to spin into a variegated yarn. If the fleece is muddy, soak it in a pail of very hot water. After an hour or two, squeeze out the excess water. The fleece will still be greasy, as it has not been treated with a detergent. Rinse once or twice in warm water, then spread the fleece to dry.

Fine wools have grease throughout the locks and need to be washed well, or the grease will resist the dye and the colors will be pale. The important points in washing wool are to use plenty of hot water and detergent and to handle the wool as little, and as gently, as possible. Fill a large container with the hottest water from the tap and add detergent. I prefer Amway's L.O.C. to other cleaning products. It cleans well, rinses out completely, and doesn't influence the color. It is available throughout the United States and Canada. Many spinners use liquid dishwashing detergents or Orvus paste, a detergent sold at farm stores that was designed for shampooing animals. Whatever product you use, the amount required depends on how hard your water is and how greasy the fleece is. Start by adding enough to make generous suds.

Push the fleece under the water (otherwise, it tends to float). When washing large amounts of fleece, add it to the pot by handfuls so that it becomes wetted uniformly. Let it soak for an hour or two. If you must leave it longer, cover the pot to keep the heat in. It won't hurt the wool to soak for more than two hours; however, when the water gets cold, the grease congeals and sticks back onto the fleece.

To test whether the wool is clean after the soaking period, plunge your fingers into the wet fleece and then touch your fingertips with your thumb. If they stick together, the wool is still greasy. Rewash,

If you want your yarn to take the dye uniformly, you must wash all the spinning oils out of it before mordanting and dyeing. Of course, mottled yarns can be quite pretty, too.

using more detergent. Spin out the sudsy water and rinse by handfuls with comfortably warm water. Spread the clean fleece by handfuls in the sun on a rack or sheet and turn it every hour. As soon as it is dry, pack it loosely in well-labeled paper or cloth bags.

Loose fiber, especially fine wool, tends to mat and thus must be handled very carefully. I have dyed more than fifty pounds of fleece at a time and not matted a single lock by avoiding sudden changes of temperature and handling the fleece as little as possible. One way to minimize handling is by combining mordant and dyestuff in the same bath, but this strategy is not always feasible; certain colors or dyeplants require that the fiber be premordanted (mordanted in a separate step before it goes into the dyebath).

PREPARING YARN FOR DYEING

Any kind of yarn—wool, mohair, silk, cotton, etc.—can be dyed with natural dyes. The first step is to wind the yarn into skeins and to secure them with four to six figure-eight ties. Choose ties that are white or colorfast—you don't want color bleeding onto the skeins—and fasten them loosely so that all parts of the yarn will have equal access to the dye liquid. But tie them well; tangled yarn, if it can be salvaged at all, takes forever to undo, especially if it's very fine. Silk is slippery and a notorious tangler; wool is troublefree by comparison.

All yarn should be washed before dyeing. Mill-spun wool yarn needs to be washed thoroughly. The factories put oil into it that makes it resist dyes, not as the natural grease does but very unpredictably. Enter well-tied skeins into a pail of hot soapy water, let soak for an hour or two, spin, rinse, and hang skeins to dry.

I like to wash and mordant a lot of fiber at once so it will be ready
for one of my marathon "dye" days.

Silk yarn is difficult to wet, and requires at least an hour's soak in hot soapy water. You can tell it's thoroughly wetted when it sinks below the surface of the water. Rinse well.

Cotton and linen yarns need special treatment to remove gums and waxes that coat the fibers and resist dyes. Fill a pot with hot water and add some soap or detergent and washing soda (start with a spoonful of soda, according to the hardness of the water). Put in the yarn, heat, and simmer for one hour. The water will get quite dirty and smell bad. Rinse the fiber several times until the rinse water runs clear.

Most handspun yarns can be washed in a pail of hot soapy water. Let the skeins soak for about an hour, spin, rinse, and dry. You can get an interesting shaded yarn by dyeing skeins handspun in the grease. Spin a thick-and-thin yarn, and the grease trapped in the overspun thin parts will resist the dye more than in the less twisted thick parts. To remove the dirt but retain the grease in yarn like this, just wash it in plain hot water.

PREPARING YARDAGE

The main concern in dyeing yardage is using a big enough dyepot. Consider the size of your dyepot when planning how much cloth to dye at once. The fabric must be able to move freely in the water.

All yardage needs to be washed before dyeing to ensure an even color. Even if you have woven the material yourself from previously washed yarn, wash it anyway; handling the yarn and fabric during weaving may have soiled it. Soak the cloth for an hour in hot soapy water, pushing it below the surface several times. Spin out the soapy water, rinse thoroughly, spin well, and hang to dry.

WEIGHING THE FIBER

In my system of dyeing, the weights of the dyestuff and mordant are calculated from the weight of the fiber whether fleece, yarn, or fabric. For example, to dye some fleece a certain shade of blue with indigo, I might first weigh out 100 grams of clean, dry fleece. If the shade of blue I wanted required a 1 percent solution of Saxon blue, I would measure out 1 percent of the weight of the fiber (100

grams), or 1 gram of indigo solution.

Weighing the fiber is the first step. When dyeing fleece, I found that 100-gram lots are a convenient size, and starting with 100 grams makes calculating percentages very simple. (Of course, you may use smaller or larger lots, depending on the size of your dyepot and the amount of each color you want to make.) It's a good idea to plan ahead and put weighed-out lots in labeled paper bags. I always weigh out twice as much as I think I'll need so I'll be prepared in case I have time for an additional run. If I'm going to dye unwashed fleece, I just go ahead and weigh it. Otherwise, I wash and dry the fleece before weighing it.

Because skeins of yarn and pieces of fabric vary in weight, you'll have to weigh and label each one. For waterproof tags, I recommend using masking tape and waterproof markers. You can weigh yarn or fabric either before you wash it or after it has dried, but record which you've done in case you want to reproduce the color later.

PLANNING FOR A PROJECT

Let's say you would like to knit a sweater or weave a scarf from your dyed fiber or yarn. It's extremely important to prepare, wash, mordant, and dye all the fiber at the same time so that it will be of one color. To be on the safe side, dye more fiber than you think you'll need.

SOAKING THE FIBER BEFORE DYEING

Wetting a fiber thoroughly before putting it into the dyepot helps it absorb the dye quickly and evenly. If you're dyeing unwashed fleece, start soaking it an hour or so before the dyebath will be ready, using hot water so as to minimize the shock when it goes into the hot dye-

Here, I've finished dyeing the darker cochineal colors,
and am preparing to dye some blues.

bath. I find that soaking fiber in hot water and then putting it in a hot dye-bath also speeds up the dyeing process. If the fiber has been washed and subsequently dried, you'll still need to soak it but only until it is fully wet. Squeeze the excess water out by hand; spinning it out cools the fiber dramatically, canceling the warming effect of the soaking.

It's most efficient to start soaking a new lot as soon as you put a lot into the dye-pot. This eliminates having an empty dyepot during your dye session. Thus, you'll soak the first fibers to be dyed while preparing the first dyebath. As soon as they go into the dyepot, you'll begin soaking the second lot, and so forth, until all the fiber has been soaked and dyed.

These yarns have been premordanted and can now be dyed or stored for future use.

M O R D A N T I N G

Mordanting is the process of preparing the fiber to receive the dyestuff. In this process, the mordant, usually a metallic salt, combines chemically with the fiber. Various substances have been used as mordants in the past; the most common ones used today are compounds of aluminum, tin, iron, copper, and chrome. All are sold in crystal or powder form and dissolved in water for use. In most cases, the fiber is simmered in the mordant bath for an hour or so.

Without a mordant, most natural dyestuffs (called adjective dyes) produce at best a light color, and this color may fade further when the dyed fiber is washed or exposed to sunlight. By contrast, applying a mordant to fibers allows these dyes to give deep, vibrant colors that are fast to washing and sunlight. Using different mordants may produce different colors from the same dyestuff. For example, logwood with no mordant gives gray. With a tin mordant, it gives pink, alum produces bluish shades, and chrome makes maroon.

A smaller group of dyestuffs (called substantive dyes), including acidic ones such as sumac and black walnuts, require no mordanting. However, using mordants with these dyes can vary or intensify the colors and improve the fastness. Indigo belongs to a special category called vat dyes, and does not require a mordant.

When to mordant

Fiber can be mordanted at three stages in the dyeing process: before, during, or after the color is applied. When to mor-

dant depends on what form the fiber is in, what dyes you're using, and what colors you want.

Premordanting, the most commonly used method, consists of mordanting the fiber before it goes into the dyepot. I use this method for yarn or yardage but not for loose fleece or fiber: the extra handling tends to result in matting and tangling. Premordanting cloth or fiber also produces the best colorfastness.

Premordanting can be done at any time before dyeing, even days or weeks in advance; premordanted fiber can be dried and stored until you're ready to use it.

Mordant baths can be reused several times, adding small amounts of additional mordant each time. Reusing the hot bath saves money and time. However, you should replace any mordant bath as soon as it starts to look unclean or muddy.

If you have only one pot to do mordanting in (you can use the same pot for all your mordanting and dyeing, if you clean it well after each use), I recommend that you choose one mordant and process your fiber in batches until you have prepared enough fiber with that particular mordant. Then scrub out the pot and prepare all the fiber wanted with another mordant. Continue in this way until you have mordanted all the fiber you need. Even if you have more than one pot, preparing a large amount of fiber ahead of time gets the less exciting and colorful steps out of the way so that you can turn your entire attention to the fun part: dyeing. Of course, you can always mordant and dye a single batch of fiber if that's all you need or want at one time.

Mordanting in the dyebath is the method I use if I am going to dye loose fiber, as it requires the least amount of handling the fleece. I hardly stir it at all, just push it by handfuls below the surface of the prepared dyebath/mordant solution. Not all dyestuffs produce fast colors when this method is used, but some can. It's especially good for extending the range of colors that can be achieved from black walnuts, cochineal, and indigo (which also produce beautiful, vibrant colors without any mordant). The colors I make this way usually come out mottled because of varying amounts of grease in different parts of the locks. They are excellent for blending and carding, and make gorgeous yarn.

Postmordanting, that is, mordanting after the fiber has been dyed, is usually done to alter the color slightly, but it is sometimes done to set the color if this wasn't achieved by premordanting or mordanting in the dyebath. Postmordanting is done in separate baths to ensure that the dyepot remains pure, thus leaving open all options of what to do next with that particular dyebath.

Three types of postmordanting treatments are blooming, greening, and saddening. These solutions are often called afterbaths. The color change in a postmordant or afterbath takes place very quickly. Only a few minutes of simmering are required.

Blooming is an old method of brightening a color with a bath containing a small amount of tin—about .25 percent (1/4 of 1 percent). I often add the tin directly to the dyebath.

Greening brings out the green tones of a color by adding a small amount of copper—about 2 percent of the weight of the fiber.

Saddening refers to darkening or dulling a color with a bath of iron. Only a very small amount of iron—no more than 2 percent of the weight of the fiber—should be used, as too much causes the fiber to deteriorate. If you look at an old Persian rug, you'll see that the dark-colored yarns are very thin or barely present; that's the effect of too much iron.

Though not technically a mordant, a hot solution of ammonia can also be used as an afterbath to change the color of a dye. Simmering is not required. The color changes almost as soon as you dip in the fiber.

USING MORDANTS EFFECTIVELY AND SAFELY

Some dyers advocate using large amounts of mordants with the idea of economizing by using less dyestuff. My method is to use less mordant and more dyestuff, as I have found that too much of some mordants, particularly tin and iron, makes fiber stiff and harsh. Too much alum makes wool, mohair, or silk feel sticky.

For these reasons and because some mordants can be harmful in other ways, I strongly urge you to use the least amount of mordant necessary. Like other chemicals such as bleach, disinfectants, gasoline, garden fertilizers, and pesticides, mordants should be treated with caution and respect. To protect yourself and those about you, follow these simple safety precautions:

▪ Label mordant containers well and store them out of the reach of children and pets.

- Wear rubber gloves to avoid skin contact with mordants.

- Wear a face mask when weighing mordant powders to avoid inhaling the dust.

- Work in a well-ventilated area.

- Never use the same measuring spoons or pots for mordanting (or dyeing) as for cooking.

MORDANT RECIPES

Mordants are measured as a percentage of the weight of the fiber to be mordanted. As mordants are very powerful, and a bit too much can make your fiber sticky, harsh, or weak, accurate weighing is a must. Remember to account for the weight of the paper or cup that you put on the scales to hold the mordant. After weighing, dissolve the mordant by stirring it in a small container of hot water; then pour this solution into the large pot of water and stir again before adding the fiber. Soaking the fiber in warm water until it is thoroughly warmed and wetted, then squeezing out the excess water before immersing it in the mordant bath ensures that the mordanting will proceed quickly and evenly. After premordanting, wash and rinse the fiber well and hang it to dry if you are not going to dye it immediately.

Different fibers require different strategies for mordanting. The first group of recipes are for mordanting wool, mohair, and other protein fibers such as alpaca or angora, and silk. Recipes for mordanting flax, cotton, ramie, or other plant fibers follow at the end of the chapter.

Mordanting with alum and tartaric acid. Alum is the mordant I use most often, but I use less than most dye books call for. Using too much alum can make wool (particularly greasy wool) feel very sticky, and the stickiness won't wash away. When I reduced the amount of alum in a typical recipe from 25 percent to 10 percent of the weight of the fiber and added 5 percent tartaric acid, I eliminated the stickiness.* At the same time, I've found that 10 percent alum is enough to produce bright colors with good fastness.

Weigh your fiber, then weigh 10 percent of the fiber weight of alum and 5 percent of tartaric acid. Dissolve them in a small container of hot water. Fill your mordant pot with water and heat it until it is warm. *Stir in the dissolved mordant, add warm, wetted fiber, bring the water to a boil, and simmer (190°F/90°C) for an hour.* Cool the fiber in the bath or remove it while still hot; spin out excess water, wash, and rinse. To reuse the bath, weigh 5 percent alum and 2.5 percent tartaric acid, dissolve them in hot water, and add to the pot. Repeat from * to *.

Tin. Weigh your fiber, then weigh out .5 percent (1/2 of 1 percent) of tin (for example, to mordant 100 grams of yarn, you would weigh out .5 gram of tin). Dissolve the tin crystals in a small container of hot water. Fill your mordant pot with water and heat it until it is warm. *Stir in the dissolved mordant, add warmed, wetted fiber, bring the water to a boil, and simmer for an hour.* Cool the fiber in the bath or remove it while still hot; spin out excess water, wash, and rinse. To reuse the bath, weigh .25 percent (1/4 of 1 percent) tin (.25 gram in the example above), dissolve it in hot water, and add to the pot. Repeat from * to *.

---

*Although I have experimented with adding other acids, I have not found any of them as beneficial as tartaric acid. Sulfuric acid dulls the color; citric acid doesn't soften and dissolves less readily than tartaric acid, resulting in less vibrant colors. Used by itself, tartaric acid has little effect on color; its primary role is to soften the fiber.

Chrome. I don't recommend this mordant; I use it only to demonstrate to my students what colors it can produce. If you decide to use chrome, handle it with care, as it is very toxic. Weigh your fiber, then weigh out 3 percent chrome. Dissolve the chrome in a small container of hot water. Fill your mordant pot with water and heat it until it is warm. *Stir in the dissolved mordant, add warmed, wetted fiber, bring the water to a boil, and simmer for an hour.* Remove the fiber; spin out excess water, wash, and rinse. To reuse the bath, weigh 1.5 percent chrome, dissolve it in hot water, and add to the pot. Repeat from * to *. This bath can be reused indefinitely.

Copper. Copper is used to bring out the green color in a dyestuff. I recommend using no more than 2 percent to ensure that the fiber doesn't become harsh. Copper may be added to the dyepot (for instance, with logwood), or a copper pot may be used as a mordanting vessel. If you choose the latter course, let the fiber cool down in the pot and stand overnight so that it will absorb as much copper as possible.

Copper is used most commonly as a postmordant for "greening" colors. In this case, simmer the fiber for five minutes in a 2 percent copper sulfate solution or for an hour in plain water in a copper pot. When premordanting with copper sulfate, simmer the fiber for one hour. I rarely use copper as a premordant, however.

Iron. An iron mordant can be used to produce a dull, or "sad", color. I recommend using no more than 2 percent to ensure that the fiber doesn't become harsh. Iron may be added to the dyepot (for instance, with sumac, as shown on page 100), or an iron pot may be used as a mordanting vessel. If you choose the latter course, let the fiber cool down in the pot and stand overnight so that it will absorb as much iron as possible.

Iron is most useful as a postmordant. In this case, simmer the fiber for five minutes in a 2 percent iron solution or for an hour in plain water in an iron pot. I rarely use iron as a premordant.

Ammonia bath. Ammonia is sometimes used as an afterbath to change the color of a dye by changing the pH of the dyebath from acid to alkaline. For example, fiber which has been dyed in an acid cochineal dyebath changes instantly from red to blue-purple when stirred in an ammonia dip. To a pail of the hottest water from the tap, add 1/2 cup of household ammonia from a freshly opened bottle. Enter the warm, wetted, dyed fiber, stir it around, and take it out. (Ammonia loses strength by evaporation on standing. If the color of the fiber doesn't change right away when you place it in the bath, add more ammonia or open a new bottle.)

MORDANTING COTTON AND LINEN

I've included only a few samples of dyed cotton and linen in this book, but many more possibilities exist. I work with cotton, linen, and other plant fibers less than I do with wool, mohair, or silk because I live in a cold climate. However, I often hear from quilters who want to use natural dyes on cotton fabrics, and at workshops in places such as California and Florida I meet spinners and weavers who want to use natural dyes on cotton.

The first step in dyeing cotton or linen is washing it thoroughly by simmering it for one hour in a big pot of water with soap or detergent and a spoonful or so of washing soda added. Rinse thoroughly before mordanting. I use only alum or alum plus tara powder (a fluffy tan powder that's very high in tannic acid, made by grinding seedpods of the tropical tree *Caesalpinia spinosa*). Mordanting cotton or linen requires more alum than I would use for wool, mohair, or silk, but these quantities don't seem to harm these plant fibers. Here are the three recipes I use.

1. Premordanting with 20 percent alum. This method is best for light, clear colors. Weigh your fiber, then weigh out 20 percent alum and dissolve it in a small container of hot water. Fill mordant pot with water and heat it until is warm. *Stir in the dissolved mordant, add warm, wetted fiber, bring the water to a boil, and simmer for one hour.* Remove the fiber; spin out excess water, wash, and rinse. To reuse the bath, weigh out 10 percent alum, dissolve it in hot water, and add to the pot. Repeat from * to *.

2. Premordanting with 20 percent alum and 10 percent tara powder in one bath. This is a convenient, all-purpose mordant for cotton or linen. Weigh your fiber, then weigh out 20 percent alum and dissolve it in a small container of hot water. Weigh out 10 percent tara powder and put it loosely into a nylon stocking. Fill your mordant pot with water. *Add the dissolved alum and the stocking of tara powder, bring the water to a boil, and simmer for one hour. Remove the stocking of tara powder. Enter warm, wetted fiber, heat, and simmer for one hour.* Remove the fiber; spin out excess water, wash, and rinse. To reuse the bath, weigh out 10 percent alum and 5 percent tara powder, dissolve the alum in hot water, and place the tara powder loosely in a stocking. Repeat from * to *.

3. Premordanting with 15 percent alum and 15 percent tara powder in two steps. This technique is best for the darkest colors, but it requires two separate solutions. The fiber is simmered first in alum solution, then in tara powder solution. This is most efficient if you have two pots. You can use just one, but the process will take longer.

Weigh your fiber, then weigh out 15 percent alum and dissolve it in a small container of hot water. Fill your mordant pot with water and heat it until it is warm. *Add the dissolved alum and stir well, then add warm, wetted fiber, bring the water to a boil, and simmer for one hour.* Remove the fiber; spin out excess water, and rinse. If you have only one mordant pot, discard the alum solution or pour it into a plastic pail to save it for later use.

Weigh out 15 percent tara powder and put it loosely into a nylon stocking. Fill a mordant pot with water, **add the stocking, bring the water to a boil, and simmer for one hour.** The tara powder solution can be simmering in a second pot while the fiber is simmering in the alum solution.) Remove the stocking, and put in the fiber which was just simmered in alum. Heat and simmer for one hour. Remove the fiber; spin out excess water, wash, and rinse.

To reuse the alum solution, weigh out 7.5 percent alum and dissolve it in hot water. Repeat from * to *. To reuse the tara powder solution, weigh out 7.5 percent tara powder and place it in a stocking. Repeat from ** to **.

TARA POWDER

TIN

ALUM

CHROME

TANNIC ACID
(can be used in place of tara powder)

IRON

COPPER

TARTARIC ACID
(cream of tartar)

Common mordants used in natural dyeing to assist the bonding of pigment to fiber.
Iron, copper, and most especially chrome are toxic and must be handled carefully.

Alum (potassium aluminum sulfate) is a white powder used as an ingredient of pickles, deodorants, and fertilizers. Nevertheless, treat it with respect. Inhaling the dust may irritate the respiratory system. Ingesting it may irritate the mouth, throat, and stomach, and in large doses, may cause diarrhea. If ingested, drink water, induce vomiting, and call the doctor. Contact with skin and eyes can cause burning; flush with plenty of water for at least 15 minutes, and call the doctor. Leftover alum mordant baths can be poured on the ground; aluminum sulfate is sold in garden stores to acidify the soil for growing blueberries, rhododendrons, and many other plants.

Tartaric acid, also called cream of tartar, is often used in combination with alum. It is a white crystalline powder produced naturally by fruits such as grapes and used in combination with baking soda as a leavening agent. Avoid inhaling any dust. A strong solution can irritate the skin; wash it off immediately with soapy water. It is safe to dispose of tartaric acid solutions by pouring the fluid on the ground; it does not harm plants or animals.

Tin (stannous chloride) is nontoxic to humans. However, when it is dissolved in water, it gives off chlorine gas, which can irritate the eyes, nose, and skin. Be sure your workplace is well ventilated. Weak tin mordant baths can be poured on the ground, well away from gardens, wells, septic tanks, and children's play areas. The chlorine will evaporate, leaving a low concentration of tin, which is not poisonous.

Iron (ferrous sulfate) is a greenish powder used in iron supplements commonly taken by children and women. Although needed by our bodies in minute amounts, iron is toxic and even fatal; children have died from accidentally eating iron tablets. A complication is that iron accumulates in the body and is not excreted. If ingested, drink plenty of milk, induce vomiting, and call the doctor immediately. Nose, eye, or skin contact with the dust can cause irritation; flush with copious amounts of water. Plants need iron, and ferrous sulfate is often sold as a soil conditioner, particularly for broad-leaved evergreens. It is safe to dispose of iron mordant baths by pouring them on the soil.

Copper in the form of copper sulfate is commonly used as a garden fungicide, even by organic gardeners. It is also used to kill algae in ponds and reservoirs. If ingested, it causes severe vomiting. Call a doctor immediately. Skin contact can result in irritation. Flush well with plenty of water. A used copper mordant bath can be poured on the ground, away from wells, septic tanks, and creeks or ponds.

Chrome (potassium dichromate) is the most toxic of the mordants used in natural dyeing. As little as 0.5 gram can cause kidney failure, coma, and convulsions, and 6 to 8 grams, death. Inhaling the powder can cause respiratory problems and lung cancer. Prolonged skin contact causes rashes and skin ulcers. Consult a doctor immediately.

The hazard to the environment of disposing chrome mordant is controversial, yet there is little need to dispose of it at all if you reuse it as I do. Save any used chrome mordant bath and store it in a tightly lidded and clearly labeled plastic pail, away from pets and children. You can reuse the bath indefinitely, adding more chrome each time.

These bright crimsons come from cochineal with a tin premordant. I like to dye a lot of different kinds of yarn and fiber at once, and combine them in my weaving.

MY APPROACH
TO DYEING

USING BOTH LOCAL AND EXOTIC DYES

Any substance that can color a fiber permanently and that occurs in nature is a natural dye. Most dyes come from plant parts such as roots, barks, leaves, flowers, seeds, or nuts. Wherever you live, there are dyes you can find locally. I call these local dyes. Onion skins, flowers from the garden or fields, and black walnut shells are common local dyestuffs.

Most local dyes produce yellow, greenish, and beige colors. For example, goldenrod produces yellows, sumac makes beige, and black walnuts give browns. Different parts of plants may produce slightly different shades; however, the differences are so slight that when I need large quantities of a dyestuff, I usually use the entire plant.

Although they are readily available, local dyes have some drawbacks. Often large quantities are required—it takes about a dozen marigold plants to produce enough flowers to dye a pound of wool. Another problem is that some local dyes are not fast, even if used with mordants. Most limiting of all is the narrow color range; local dyes give too many yellows and tans and almost no reds, purples, or blues.

Fleece dyed in a range of shades is fun to blend in handspun yarns. I do most of my dyeing in the summer, and then spin all winter.

45

Because I want to produce a wide range of beautiful, intense colors, I also use dyes produced in other parts of the world, often in tropical regions, and sold in North America by local and mail-order fibercraft businesses. These exotic dyes are often more concentrated than local dyes, and they are more permanent. Some of my favorites are cochineal, which gives pinks, reds, and purples; indigo for blue; logwood for pinks, blues, maroons, and grays; madder for oranges and reds; and sandalwood for burnt orange and browns.

MAKING CONCENTRATED DYEBATHS

I've been very pleased with the results I get by using generous amounts of dyestuff to make concentrated dyebaths. When working with fresh local dye plants, I usually weigh out ten times the weight of the fiber. With dry local plants, I use four times the weight of the fiber. Most of the exotic dyes are stronger so less of them is required. (See chapter VII for more specific information on each dye.)

Starting with a concentrated dyebath makes it possible to get very intense colors. It also allows you to reuse the same bath as many as eight to ten times for a series of lighter and lighter shades. A reused dyebath is usually called an exhaust bath.

MIXING DYES

Using a variety of local and exotic dyes gives many different colors, but mixing dyes—combining them in the same dyepot—produces an even wider range of beautiful colors. This technique differs from topdyeing or overdyeing, in which the fiber is dyed first in one dyebath and then in another. Compared to topdyeing, mixing dyes has two main advantages: it

saves time, and by handling the fiber less, matting and tangling are minimized.

I used to dye 400 pounds of yarn every summer for a local production weaver. He needed to have the upcoming fashion colors, and I was able to make them from natural dyes. In fact, I used the same assortment of dyes to make thirty to forty different colors each year. I created several of the colors by mixing dyes.

For example, adding a little cochineal to a marigold dyebath gives oranges. Mixing the Saxon blue indigo solution with a marigold or goldenrod dyebath gives lovely greens. Mixing red sandalwood with black walnut produces a warm reddish brown. Combining exotics with the local dyes, especially the yellow dyes which are so plentiful in most areas, greatly expands the range of colors you can get and sometimes improves the fastness as well.

Mixing is also a good way to use exhaust baths. For example, there's still valuable color in a cochineal dyebath even after it

Black walnuts are free for the gathering, and make lovely brown tones that can be used alone or mixed with other dyes.

has been used so many times that it just gives light pink. Mixing some of that cochineal exhaust bath into a black walnut dyebath makes warm reddish browns.

Often I approach a dye project by thinking first about the colors that I want to get, then asking myself how I can make them. For example, to dye wool or mohair for doll hair, I could use cutch or black walnut. Used alone, they give different shades of brown, but I can get similar hues by mixing either with small amounts of madder or sandalwood. I can choose one or another dye or dye combination according to what I have available at the time, and what other dyeing I want to do on the same day.

Although I prefer mixing, in some cases topdyeing does give better results. In particular, I like to use a logwood exhaust bath with copper mordant to dye fiber blue, then topdye that fiber in a marigold or goldenrod dyebath for shades of green.

OTHER WAYS TO MULTIPLY THE COLORS

There are many ways to increase the range of colors that you get from natural dyes. One idea is to start with fibers of different colors, such as natural gray instead of white wool. These produce heathery shades. Another is to use different fibers, such as wool from different breeds of sheep, or mohair, silk, or other fibers. Even in the same dyepot, different fibers take on slightly different colors. Premordanting the fiber with different mordants or using different postmordants or afterbaths can produce strikingly different colors from the same dyebath. By combining all these techniques, you can end up with many colors from a single dyepot.

Next to mohair, silk is my favorite fiber to dye because of the richness of the colors and sheen of the fibers.

Part of a day's work—many shades of pink, blue, red, and purple.

TIPS FOR EFFICIENT DYEING

Because I live in a cold climate and work outdoors, I need to do a whole year's worth of dyeing in a single season—summer. For many years, I dyed hundreds of pounds of yarn and fleece each summer. This situation forced me to develop practical and efficient methods of dyeing! I usually dye large quantities—as much as twenty-four or fifty pounds of fiber at a time—but the following tips save time and money even if you just want to dye small amounts of fleece or yarn.

■ Prepare your fiber in advance. Wash and dry fleece, and weigh it into convenient portions, such as 100-gram units. Make yarn into skeins and tie them securely. Make all the skeins the same size, such as 25 turns around the skein winder or niddy-noddy. Make a note of how much the average skein weighs, so you'll be able to figure how much mordant and dyestuff to use. Wash the yarn.

It's easy to see why I love dyeing with cochineal—
the colors are simply breathtaking.

■ Set up a mordant bath and use it over and over to premordant a big supply of yarn. As soon as you remove one batch of yarn, add more mordant to the hot liquid and put in more yarn. It saves time (and fuel) to reuse water that's already simmering instead of heating up a new potful. Mordant more than you think you need—chances are you'll use it after all. Label the premordanted skeins to indicate which mordant bath was used.

■ Make concentrated dyebaths that you can reuse for several exhaust baths.

■ Soak the fiber in hot water until it's thoroughly warm and wet before putting it into the dyepot. Soaking prepares the fiber to receive the dye quickly and evenly.

■ Keep the dyepot occupied. Never let it sit empty. As soon as you remove one batch of fiber, put in the next. While one batch is being dyed, the next batch should be soaking in preparation.

Getting all the tools, fibers, dyepots, and afterbaths organized ahead of time is essential to a successful workshop or production dyeing experience.

MANY COLORS FROM A FEW POTS:

A DYE WORKSHOP

This chapter describes how I organize a three-day dye workshop for twenty participants. You might like to follow a similar approach to plan a special weekend event with some friends from your guild or study group, or a marathon dye session for yourself. Expect to spend a few days on preparation before the workshop starts. The workshop itself includes three days of dyeing and two evenings of compiling sample cards.

The goals of the workshop are (1) to make as many colors as possible, (2) to weigh the fibers and dyes accurately and keep careful records so that you can reproduce any of the colors, and (3) to use the dyebaths completely, in a controlled manner. At the end of the workshop, each participant takes home twenty different color cards with twenty-four shades on each card, up to a pound of dyed wool or mohair fleece, and a sample of one particular color that was selected from the samples and reproduced. If you do this as a solo project, you'll end up with a set of sample cards for future reference, plus enough dyed yarn to last a long time!

The sample cards will be a valuable resource for future reference. They will give you the opportunity to choose from many colors and the directions for how to reproduce each one. On each card, the colors will be varied and yet compatible. It would be fun to use larger quantities of yarn and make all twenty-four shades from one or two dye recipes, then use the yarn to knit a sweater with a design in it or to weave a tapestry.

WORKING IN TEAMS

When I teach workshops, I like to divide the participants into teams of two, pairing beginners or less experienced dyers with more experienced dyers. There are several advantages to working in teams. More people can learn with less equipment, and it's more fun to work with some else than alone. Partners can help each other by discussing each step, double-checking the calculations, and monitoring the dyepots. Making the sample cards in the evenings is a big project, but it seems to go a lot faster working in teams.

FACILITY AND EQUIPMENT

I think it's best to do this workshop outdoors. If you must work inside, be sure there is a good exhaust system, not just a fan here or there. If there isn't a built-in system, check the Yellow Pages for sources where you can rent an industrial exhaust system. (Good ventilation is important for all dye workshops, not just for natural dye workshops.)

There should be convenient access to running water, including hot running water if possible, and a drain for disposing of wash and rinse water and used baths.

For every team of two participants, you'll need

❖ 1 dyepot

❖ 1 stove

❖ 3 or 4 small plastic pails or containers that will hold about two liters (one-half gallon) or more.

❖ 1 or 2 wooden dowels or stirring sticks

❖ Thermometer to monitor the dyebath temperature

❖ Rubber gloves

❖ Notebook for keeping track of what you do

❖ Pair of scissors for cutting the dyed yarn into samples

For the workshop as a whole, you'll also need

❖ at least 1 (more if possible) metric scale accurate to 0.1 gram (1/10 of 1 gram) to weigh the yarn and mordants as you prepare for the workshop and to weigh dyestuffs during the workshop

❖ If no hot running water, at least 1 more pot and stove for heating water

❖ 2 extra dyepots and stoves for post-mordanting with tin and copper; small amounts of tin and copper mordants

❖ Plastic pail and a fresh bottle of house-hold ammonia to use as an afterbath

❖ 1 or more (preferably several) salad spinners for extracting liquid from the skeins

❖ If no sink, 1 plastic dishpan with soap or detergent for washing dyed skeins

❖ Clothes-drying rack or clothesline for hanging skeins to dry

❖ Stiff cardboard sample cards with 24 holes along one edge; 1 per participant for each dye used as well as 1 or 2 extra sets for the guild scrapbook and library.

ADVANCE PREPARATION

Well before the workshop, the yarn that you will be dyeing must be wound into skeins and tied, labeled, washed, and premordanted. This is a big job—don't underestimate how long it takes. I recommend using wool, mohair, other animal fibers such as cashgora or alpaca, or silk yarns. (I don't usually include cotton in workshops because it takes a different approach and longer dyeing times.) It's more fun if you choose a variety of yarns—thick and thin, smooth and textured—as well as a variety of fibers.

For each participant, use about 100 grams (3.52 ounces) of yarn, and make it into twenty-four skeins. Each skein should weigh a bit more than 4 grams. Make a sample first to see how many times you have to wind the yarn around your niddy-noddy or skein reel to make a 4-gram skein, and then make the rest of the skeins with the same number of turns.

Tie the two loose ends of each skein together, wrapping them loosely around the skein, and use white yarn or string to tie the skein loosely in at least two or three other places. Fold a piece of waterproof masking tape or freezer tape over the yarn ends to serve as a label, and number the skeins from 1 to 24 with a waterproof marker or pen. Bundle the skeins in four groups: 1 to 6, 7 to 12, 13 to 18, and 19 to 24. Secure each bundle with a few loose ties and attach a tape label to one of the ties. Weigh the bundle and record the weight on the label. Then wash the bundled skeins in hot, soapy water and rinse well.

Now the skeins are ready for premordanting (see page 39). You can premordant several bundles at a time. Add up the weights marked on each bundle to find the total weight of fiber.

❖ Use tin to premordant the skeins numbered 1 to 6. For wool or mohair, weigh tin equal to 0.5 percent (1/2 of 1 percent) of the fiber weight. For silk, use 1 percent of the fiber weight.

❖ Use alum and tartaric acid to premordant the skeins numbered 7 to 12. For all fibers, use 10 percent alum and 5 percent tartaric acid.

❖ Use chrome to premordant the skeins numbered 13 to 18. For all fibers, use 3 percent chrome. Save the used chrome mordant bath for later use by storing it in a closely sealed and clearly labeled jar or pail. (Although I rarely use chrome in my own dyeing, I include it in workshops to make a point: many of the colors you get with chrome can be obtained in other ways, but that can be demonstrated only after the colors have been made.)

❖ Do not premordant the skeins numbered 19 to 24.

After mordanting, wash all the skeins well, then group them so that numbers 1 to 24 of each kind of yarn are back together again. Check to make sure that every set is complete.

Choose some fleece to dye, also. (Participants who don't spin can share their fleece with someone who does or use it to make felt.) I recommend nice, shiny Lincoln, Coopworth, Border Leicester, or second-clip kid mohair. Natural dyes sparkle on these lustrous fibers. Include some gray or light brown fleece if you can get it. For each participant, allow about 250 to 500 grams (about 1/2 to 1 pound) of fleece. You don't need to premordant the fleece. In fact, if it's not too muddy or greasy, you don't even need to wash it. If it is quite muddy or greasy, it's a good idea to wash it in advance. You don't have to divide the fleece into portions now; there will be time to do that during the workshop.

Looping skeins over the drying lines is quicker and more secure than using clothespins, especially when you're handling a lot of them.

PLANNING COLORS

Any recipe from this book can be used in a workshop. When I am teaching and do the preparation myself, I choose several recipes that will provide a variety of colors and obtain sufficient quantities of the dyestuffs needed. If your study group or guild plans a workshop, you could form teams in advance, and each team could sign up for two recipes, one for the first day and one for the second day. (Two or more teams can use the same recipe if

24 skeins and several samples of fleece. The chart outlines the steps the members of each team should follow. Although the tasks are divided up to make the chart more clear, you'll want to help each other, of course.

WORKSHOP DAY 3

The third day is like a test. Each participant or team chooses a color from one of the cards—not necessarily one that the team has already made—and tries to re-

Having clear procedures spelled out for workshop participants is every
bit as important as having all the materials organized.

they dye different kinds of yarn.) This approach will help you know which dyestuffs to have on hand and in what quantities. Cochineal and cochineal mixes are often favorites because the dyeing goes quickly and makes so many pretty colors.

WORKSHOP DAYS 1 AND 2

The procedure is the same on both days. Each team uses one recipe to dye a set of

produce it. It's best to use the same kind of fiber—wool, mohair, or silk—as that of the sample. Following the guidelines in this chapter and the recipe on the card, go through all the steps of washing, weighing, and premordanting (if needed) the fiber; preparing the dyebath; dyeing the fiber; and postmordanting (if needed). If the recipe was followed carefully both times, you should be able to reproduce the color of the sample.

Following the Skeins Through the Dye Workshop

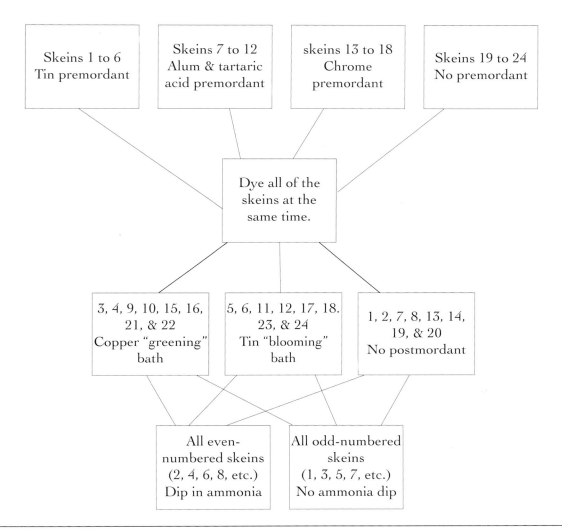

Key to the Dyed Skeins & Samples

Skein #	Pre-mordant	Post-mordant	Skein #	Pre-mordant	Post-mordant
1	Tin	none	13	Chrome	none
2	Tin	ammonia	14	Chrome	ammonia
3	Tin	copper	15	Chrome	copper
4	Tin	copper, ammonia	16	Chrome	copper, ammonia
5	Tin	tin	17	Chrome	tin
6	Tin	tin, ammonia	18	Chrome	tin, ammonia
7	Alum, tartaric acid	none	19	None	none
8	Alum, tartaric acid	ammonia	20	None	ammonia
9	Alum, tartaric acid	copper	21	None	copper
10	Alum, tartaric acid	copper, ammonia	22	None	copper, ammonia
11	Alum, tartaric acid	tin	23	None	tin
12	Alum, tartaric acid	tin, ammonia	24	None	tin, ammonia

WORKSHOP COORDINATOR OR VOLUNTEERS

Prepare the three afterbaths for the entire workshop to share. Use the average weight of a set of 24 skeins—about 100 grams—as the weight of fiber. For copper, use 2 percent of that weight (2 grams) to make a "greening" bath. For tin, use 0.5 percent (0.5 grams) to make a "blooming" bath. Mix each mordant with hot water and put the pots (labeled) on their stoves to heat. For the ammonia afterdip, pour about 1/2 cup of ammonia into a pail of hot water. Label that, too.

Note that copper, tin, and ammonia afterbaths can each be used by several teams before they will need to be renewed or replaced. There may be some transfer of color if the skeins weren't rinsed well; have the teams with light-colored yarns use the afterbaths before the teams with darker-colored yarns. You can add 1 percent (1 gram) copper or 0.25 percent (0.25 gram) tin to renew those baths, but if the liquid is very dark from dye run-off, it's better to replace it with a fresh solution.

Pour out the ammonia dip when it no longer seems to be effective, and replace it with a fresh hot solution.

ONE TEAMMATE

As soon as you arrive, weigh the 24 skeins of yarn and weigh out the required amount of dyestuff according to your recipe. Many of the recipes call for soaking the dyestuff overnight before simmering it. It's no problem to plan ahead and soak dyes for the second or third days of the workshop, but you may not be able to soak them overnight before the first day. Don't worry. If you get started early and let the dyestuff soak for an hour or so, it will work fine—it just won't yield quite as much color as it would after longer soaking. Follow the recipe and prepare the dyebath.

When the dyebath is ready, add the fiber. Heat to simmering and note the time. Check the recipe for how long to simmer the skeins and tell your teammate what time (write the time in your notebook as a reminder) the yarn is due to come out. Check occasionally that the temperature is correct and the yarn is fully immersed in the dye.

When the time comes, remove the yarn from the dyepot. Spin the skeins in the salad spinner to extract excess dye liquid and return this to the dyebath. Rinse the skeins in warm water, spin out excess water, and spread them out to cool off enough that you can handle them.

Separate the bundle of skeins and find the number tags. Take the skeins numbered 3, 4, 9, 10, 15, 16, 21, and 22 (a total of eight skeins) and put them in the copper "greening" bath. Simmer for five minutes, then remove the skeins and spin out the excess liquid. Rinse well.

Take the skeins numbered 5, 6, 11, 12, 17, 18, 23, and 24 (a total of eight skeins) and put them in the tin "blooming" bath. Simmer for five minutes, then remove the skeins and spin out the excess liquid. Rinse well.

Regroup the skeins. Now take all the even-numbered skeins (2, 4, 6, 8, etc.) and dip them in the ammonia solution. If the liquid is warm, it can indeed be just a dip—the color will change immediately. If the liquid has cooled, leave the skeins for a few minutes.

Wash all the skeins in warm soapy water and rinse them well. Hang them up to dry.

THE OTHER TEAMMATE

Soak the skeins of yarn in a pail of hot water. Push them down from time to time to make sure they get completely wetted.

Meanwhile, weigh out 100 grams of fleece (greasy or washed) and put it in a pail of hot water to soak. If your recipe calls for a mordant, weigh out the amount required so that you can add it to the dyepot and mordant the fleece at the same time as you dye it. Dissolve the mordant in a cup of warm water.

After the yarn is out of the dyebath, add the dissolved mordant (if required) to the pot and stir well. Gently squeeze excess water out of the soaked fleece and carefully lower it into the hot dyebath. Heat to simmering and note the time. Check the recipe for how long to simmer the fleece, and tell your teammate what time the fleece is due to come out (Write the time in your notebook as a reminder.) Check occasionally that the temperature is correct and the fleece is fully immersed in the dye.

Weigh out another 100 grams of fleece and put it in hot water to soak. If the recipe calls for mordant, weigh out one-half as much as you did the first time, and dissolve it in a cup of hot water.

When the time comes, remove the first bath of fleece from the dyepot. Spin it in the salad spinner to extract excess dye liquid and return this to the dyebath. Rinse the fleece in warm water and spin out the excess water.

Add the dissolved mordant for the second batch of fleece (if required) to the dyebath and stir well. Gently squeeze excess water out of the fleece and carefully lower it into the hot dyebath. Heat and simmer as before. When the time comes, remove the fleece from the dyepot and spin and rinse it.

BOTH TEAMMATES

Now it is up to you to decide what to do next. If you're using cochineal, you may be able to do as many as seven or eight exhaust baths. Other dyestuffs, such as brazilwood, may be exhausted after only two or three uses. Using 100-gram portions of fleece, try putting them in the greening, blooming, or ammonia bath to see how the color compares with yarn given the same treatment. Be sure to label all samples and record what you have done in your notebook.

You may want to mix some of your dyebath with some from another team. Keep track of whatever you do. Work with the dyebath until it is completely exhausted.

When the yarn is dry, prepare the sample cards, making one for each workshop participant. On each card, write the recipe that you used, giving a full description. Cut the skeins apart, keeping track of which is which, and put the samples (in order!) in the 24 holes along the edge of the card.

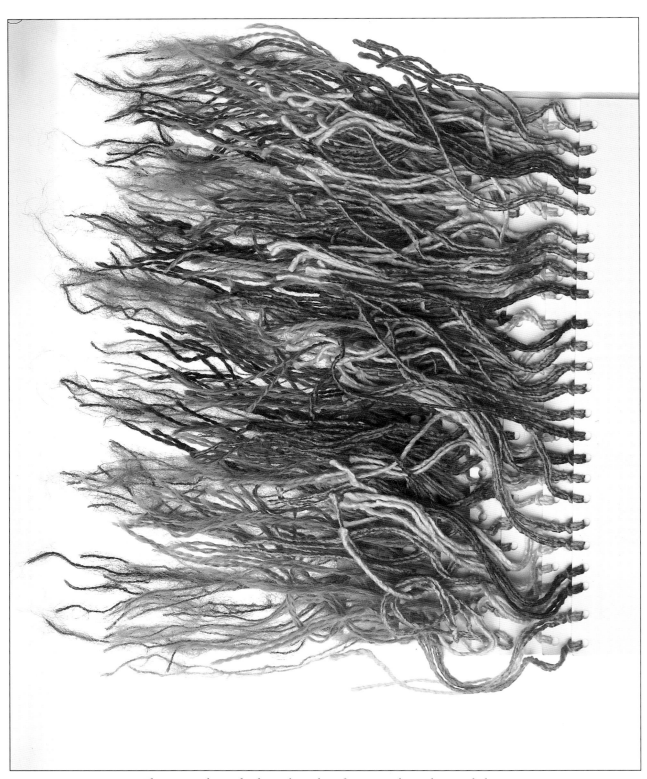

These sample cards show the colors from one three-day workshop.
Each participant gets a set of all the colors, and recipes for reproducing them.

Making the sample cards up is an important part
of the workshop, and you must allow plenty of time for it.

A PORTFOLIO
OF COLOR

THE COLORS on the following pages represent only a few of the possibilities offered by a few of my favorite dyestuffs. I hope you will use these recipes as starting points for your own color explorations. Be prepared for color variations according to the origin, age, strength, and quality of the dyes you use, the mineral content of your water, and the fibers you choose—and all the other variables that will surely arise from time to time.

Some of the colors shown were obtained by immersing different fibers, or the same fibers with different premordants, in a single dyebath for slightly different shades. Others resulted from immersing one fiber for a given length of time and then removing it, then adding new fiber to the same bath for a lighter shade, and so on until all the color was exhausted. Still others came from mixing two dyestuffs in the same bath, or dyeing a fiber first with one color, then with another. As you read the recipes for each, remember that the dyestuff percentages given refer to a percent of the

weight of the fibers, called "weight of goods", or WOG, an abbreviation you'll see used throughout the recipes.

In those cases in which a color resulted from a partially exhausted dyebath, I've indicated the number of that bath: for example, "third cochineal bath" means that two lots of fiber were previously dyed in the bath, which started at a given percentage; by the third bath, much of the dyestuff would have been used up. Different dyestuffs are used up at different rates; for instance, the second bath of cochineal is almost as intense as the first, while the second bath of brazilwood is quite pale. I've tested each of the exhaust recipes to see what percentage of dyestuff you would have to use to achieve the same color, and have given those percentages when the sample shown was dyed by that method. I've confirmed all my results with repeated testings, but you might experience variations. Keep track of these and make the information part of your permanent dye reference notebook.

THE kamala or lotus tree (*Mallotus philippinensis*) is a small tree native to southheast Asia. Its fruits yield the dyestuff kamala, an orange powder which produces brilliant yellows and oranges on wool, mohair, and silk.

Dyeing with kamala

Kamala powder will dissolve only in an alkaline solution. When you first put the measured amount of kamala powder into a dyepot of water, it will appear to be curdling. Adding washing soda makes the water alkaline enough so that the curds dissolve, making a yellow solution. I start with a teaspoonful and add more if needed depending on the initial pH of the water. Stir well. As soon as the kamala powder is dissolved, the dyebath is ready for use. Add the wetted fiber, bring the water to a boil, and simmer for one hour.

Too much washing soda makes wool feel harsh. Rinse the fiber in vinegar after dyeing to neutralize the solution and protect the fiber.

KAMALA The rich, saturated yellows of kamala have a reddish cast similar to saffron, unlike the greener yellows of many natural dyestuffs. Its colors are especially beautiful on silk.

Silk yarn, alum premordant, kamala powder at 30% WOG, washing soda at 3% WOG in bath. Vinegar afterbath to neutralize washing soda.

Same recipe as above on handspun silk-wool blend yarn.

The lighter colored silk was premordanted with tin, the darker with alum. Kamala powder at 30% WOG, washing soda at 3% WOG in bath. Vinegar afterbath to neutralize washing soda.

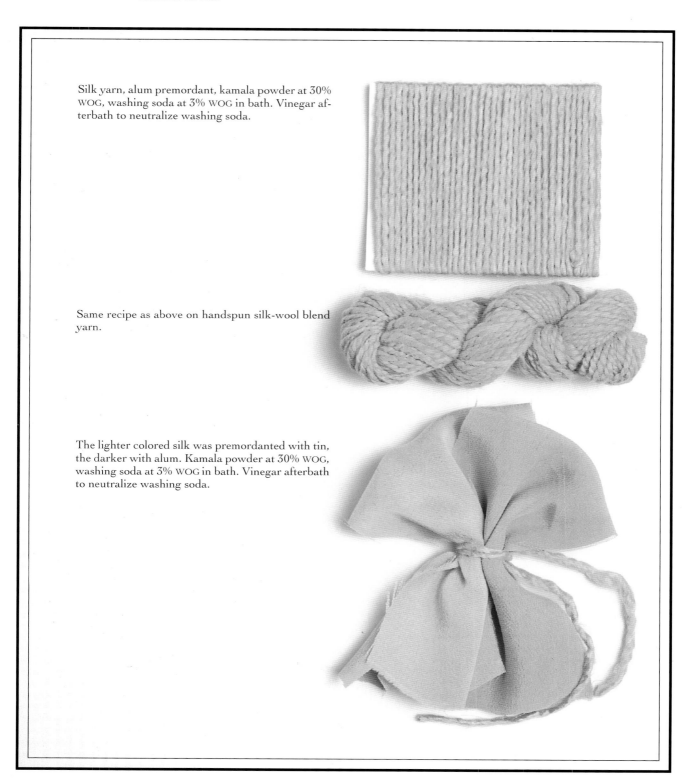

OSAGE ORANGE or bois d'arc (*Maclura pomifera*) is a spiny tree native to Arkansas and Texas but planted throughout the midwestern and northeastern United States. Its wood is a bright golden yellow and makes a very clear lemon yellow dye. The dyestuff is sold both as chips or sawdust (shown here) and as a concentrated extract.

Dyeing with Osage orange

If you're using wood chips or sawdust, weigh out as much as you need, cut chips in small pieces, then place the dyestuff in a nylon stocking. Put it in a pot, covered with water, to soak overnight. The next day, bring the water to a boil and simmer one hour, then remove the stocking of dye material from the dyebath. If using concentrate, simply measure out the required amount and dissolve it in hot water. Add the warmed, wetted fiber to the Osage orange dyebath, bring to a boil, and simmer for one hour.

OSAGE ORANGE Strong, fast yellows are produced by Osage orange. It's effective on wool and other protein fibers, and on cotton and linen as well. Osage orange combines well with other dyes; see it used to overdye logwood on page 109.

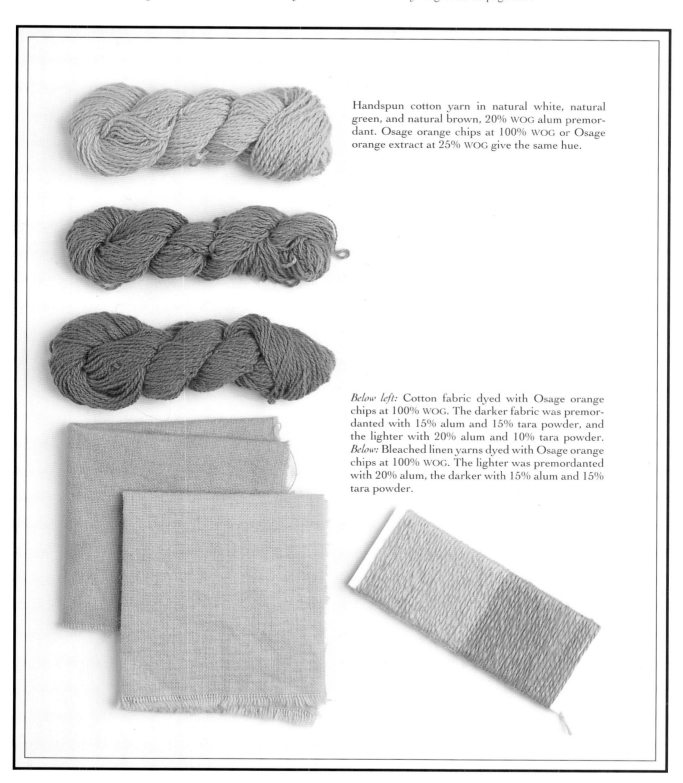

Handspun cotton yarn in natural white, natural green, and natural brown, 20% WOG alum premordant. Osage orange chips at 100% WOG or Osage orange extract at 25% WOG give the same hue.

Below left: Cotton fabric dyed with Osage orange chips at 100% WOG. The darker fabric was premordanted with 15% alum and 15% tara powder, and the lighter with 20% alum and 10% tara powder. *Below:* Bleached linen yarns dyed with Osage orange chips at 100% WOG. The lighter was premordanted with 20% alum, the darker with 15% alum and 15% tara powder.

IN ANY region, there's an abundance of local wildflowers or garden plants that produce yellow dyes. Three of my favorites are marigolds, goldenrod, and dyer's coreopsis. They all produce similar colors whether used alone or in mixes with purchased dyes such as indigo. For fast colors, use premordanted fibers with all local yellow dyes.

Marigolds (*Tagetes* spp.) are strongly scented annuals native to Mexico and Central America and very popular as garden plants throughout North America. The yellow, orange, or red-and-yellow blossoms produce shades of yellow, orange, gold, bronze, and brown, depending on concentration and mordant. The plants are in bloom from midsummer until frost, and the more flowers you pick, the more are produced. You can use them fresh or dry them for later use.

Pick marigolds in the morning as soon as the dew has dried, then weigh them and record the weight. The percentage used for dyeing is based on the weight of the freshly picked flowers. To use them fresh, simply squeeze or bruise them a little, then put them in a dyepot of clean water to soak overnight. The next day, bring the water to a boil, simmer for one hour, and strain the dyebath into another pot. To dry marigolds, spread them in the sun, turning them from time to time to expose all sides to the sun and air. When they are crisp, store them in a paper bag marked with their original fresh weight. They can be stored for months or years and still give very good color. When you want to use the dried marigolds, soak them in warm water overnight. The next day, bring the water to a boil and simmer for one hour, then strain the dyebath into another pot. Add prepared fiber to the marigold dyebath, bring to a boil, and simmer for one hour.

Goldenrod (*Solidago canadensis*) is a native perennial that thrives in abandoned farm fields, waste places, and roadsides. It grows to 5 feet tall and has narrow, dark green leaves with plumes or clusters of bright yellow flowers between July and October. (There are dozens of species of goldenrod; all work for dyeing.) It is plentiful enough to be considered a weed in our area, but I like it anyway. It's a beautiful sight when the wind rustles through a field of blooming goldenrod, like waves on a golden sea.

Gather the flower heads for dyeing by

breaking off the tops of the upright stalks. If picked before the flowers are fully open, goldenrod gives greenish yellows and lemon-limes. Including some of the leaves adds green to the color. If you wait until full bloom, goldenrod gives yellows, golds, and oranges. For the clearest yellows, use only the flowers, not the leaves or stems.

Weigh out the required amount of flowers. Bruise or crush them and place them in a large pot of water to soak overnight. The next day, bring the water to a boil and simmer for one hour, then strain the dyebath into another pot. Enter the prepared fiber, bring the bath to a boil, and simmer for one hour.

Dyer's coreopsis (*Coreopsis tinctoria*) is an annual plant native to North America and often cultivated in gardens. It grows 2 to 3 feet tall and does best in full sun. The plant bears thin, stringy leaves and bright yellow and dark orange-red flowers. The more flowers you pick, the more that appear. The flowers, which may be used fresh or dried for dyeing, produce yellows and oranges.

Pick the flowers and weigh out the required amount for dyeing. If you're planning to dry the flowers for later use, write the fresh weight on a paper bag in which you will store the flowers when they are fully dry. To use fresh or dried flowers, crush them and soak in water overnight. The next day, bring the water to a boil, simmer for one hour, then strain the dyebath into another pot. Enter the prepared fiber, bring the bath to a boil, and simmer for one hour.

Alone, a concentrated dyebath of dyer's coreopsis gives a wonderful strong orange. Adding a little cochineal warms the color to a reddish orange.

MARIGOLD Dried marigold flowers at percentages as low as 25% of weight of goods give strong, though dull, yellows; the higher percentages shown here are more vivid and colorfast. All the samples on this page were premordanted with alum; the variable that causes the samples at left to have such a strong orange cast is the fiber: mohair seems to take the color from marigolds differently than wool or silk. You can see the same effect on fibers premordanted with tin.

Above, from the top: Three samples of brushed mohair with alum premordant. Dye percentages are 400%, 200%, and 400% WOG. Bottom sample had copper "greening" afterbath. *Below:* Wool fabric, alum premordant, dried marigold flowers at 400% and 200% WOG, respectively. Fabric on left was given an ammonia afterbath.

Above: These silk yarns were all premordanted with alum and dyed with dried marigold flowers at 400% WOG. The middle sample was given an ammonia afterbath, and the bottom one a copper afterbath. The silk fabric sample below was premordanted with alum, dyed at 400% WOG, with no afterbath.

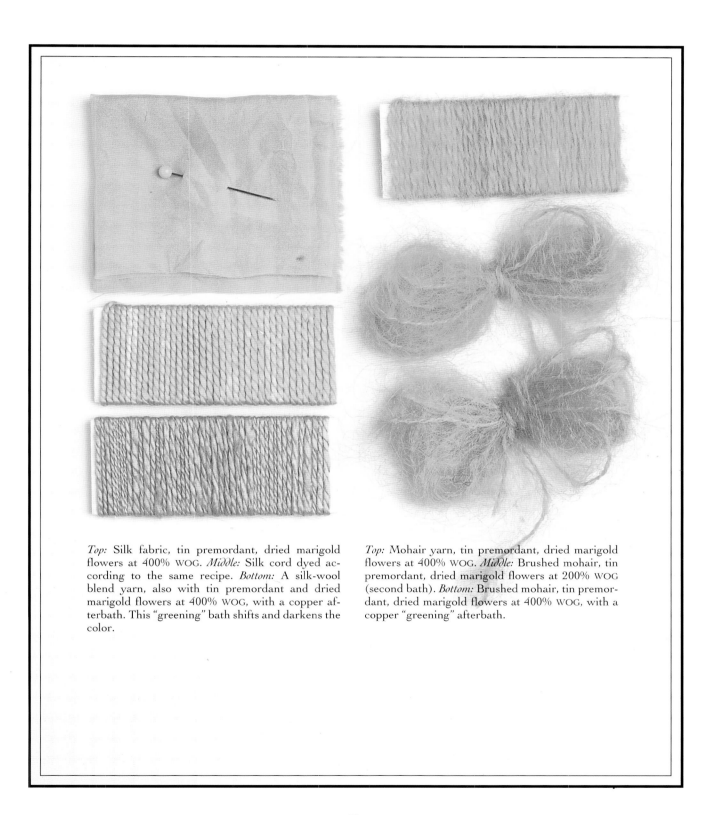

Top: Silk fabric, tin premordant, dried marigold flowers at 400% WOG. *Middle:* Silk cord dyed according to the same recipe. *Bottom:* A silk-wool blend yarn, also with tin premordant and dried marigold flowers at 400% WOG, with a copper afterbath. This "greening" bath shifts and darkens the color.

Top: Mohair yarn, tin premordant, dried marigold flowers at 400% WOG. *Middle:* Brushed mohair, tin premordant, dried marigold flowers at 200% WOG (second bath). *Bottom:* Brushed mohair, tin premordant, dried marigold flowers at 400% WOG, with a copper "greening" afterbath.

GOLDENROD The samples below were dyed with goldenrod flowers; slightly different shades will result from including foliage in the dyebath. This abundant wildflower can be found throughout North America; it blooms in late summer and early fall.

Above: Wool fleece, no mordant, dried goldenrod flowers at 400% and 250% WOG, tin aftermordant. *Below:* Brushed mohair, handspun wool, and wool fabric, all with alum premordant, dried marigold flowers at 250% WOG (second bath). The brushed mohair had a 2% WOG copper aftermordant and ammonia afterbath.

Above: Yarns dyed with dried goldenrod flowers at 400%, 400%, and 250% WOG respectively. The first sample had a 2% WOG copper aftermordant. *Below:* Mohair yarns and wool fabric, tin premordant, dried goldenrod flowers at 400% WOG.

COREOPSIS As with other local yellow recipes here, I have calculated percentages for coreopsis dyes on the dried weight of the flowers. Mordants dramatically affect the colors achieved with coreopsis; this isn't generally the case with yellow flower dyes.

Top: Brushed mohair, no mordant, dried coreopsis flowers at 400% WOG. *Middle:* Wool fabric, alum premordant, dried coreopsis flowers at 400% WOG. *Bottom:* Alpaca yarn, alum premordant, dried coreopsis flowers at 200% WOG (second bath).

These three skeins of brushed mohair were premordanted with tin and dyed with dried coreopsis flowers at 400%, 200%, and 100% WOG. Note how strong a red cast the tin mordant contributes.

PARMELIA (*Parmelia saxatilis*) is a lichen found throughout much of North America. It forms flat, crusty mats on rocks, trees, and wood, depending on the climate. The color is grayish green to grayish white with an occasional tinge of rust. It is most easily harvested when wet; then you can lift pieces with a knife. Because this lichen grows so slowly, gather only as much as you need, and never take much from any one place. Spread it out to dry; when it is completely dry, you can store it indefinitely.

Parmelia gives a variety of orangy yellows on wool and mohair, and must be used with a mordant for fastness. Smaller ratios of lichen to fiber produce tan or buff shades that are much less interesting.

Dyeing with parmelia

Parmelia, like many other lichens used for dyeing, imparts a wonderfully sweet, woodsy, almost smoky fragrance to wool that is quite persistent. For other lichen dyes, see pages 110, 111, 116, and 120. Take the required amount of dried parmelia, crush it, and soak it overnight in cold water. The next day, simmer the water at 85°C for at least one hour. Strain the dyebath into another container. Add the warmed, wetted fiber to the dyepot and simmer for one hour (or longer for darker colors).

PARMELIA LICHEN Parmelias and the orchil lichens discussed on pages 110–111 are only two of many lichens that provide interesting colors. Browns, rusts, grays, oranges, golds, and some unexpected blues and pinks come from these unlikely looking symbiotic plants.

These two samples, a woolen fabric and loop mohair yarn, were both premordanted with alum and dyed with crushed lichen at 200% WOG. Lesser percentages of lichen to fiber give uninteresting tans. While most lichens will dye fiber without a mordant, the colors tend not to be lightfast. Be careful not to let the dyebath come to a boil; 85°C is the ideal temperature for this dyestuff.

M A D D E R

MADDER (*Rubia tinctorum*) is a sprawling perennial with narrow, pointed leaves and prickly stems. It is native to the Mediterranean region and Asia Minor, and has long been used for dyeing wool, cotton, and other fibers. The roots produce a dye which gives a variety of orange-reds, oranges, browns, and brownish reds. When I first started using natural dyes, the roots I bought were thicker than the ones sold now, and they seemed to give redder colors. The madder available nowadays seems to give more orangy colors.

Madder is easy to grow in temperate climates, and the rather weedy plants will spread and produce harvestable roots in two or three growing seasons.

Dyeing with madder

Weigh out the required amount of roots.

The dry roots are very tough and hard, but try to chop or break them into smaller pieces as best you can. Put them in a dyepot of clean water, and let them soak for several hours or overnight. Heat the water no hotter than 185°F (85°C) for 30 minutes, remove the pot from the heat, and let it stand for a second night. The next day, heat the bath for one hour, keeping the temperature below 185°F (85°C). Strain the dyebath into another pot. (You can dry the roots and save them to use again for lighter colors.)

Add the premordanted, warmed, wetted fiber to the dyepot. Heat the dyebath and simmer it for one hour. Boiling at 212°F (100°C) gives shades of brown while keeping the temperature below 158°F (70°C) gives more orangy colors.

MADDER The roots of other members of the madder family—lady's bedstraw, sweet woodruff, and others—are reputed to also yield reddish dyes, and are worth experimenting with. Madder has the most abundant root system and the greatest concentration of dye pigments, though. The temperature of madder dyebaths shouldn't exceed 85°C (185°F); at higher temperatures the colors become brown and muddy.

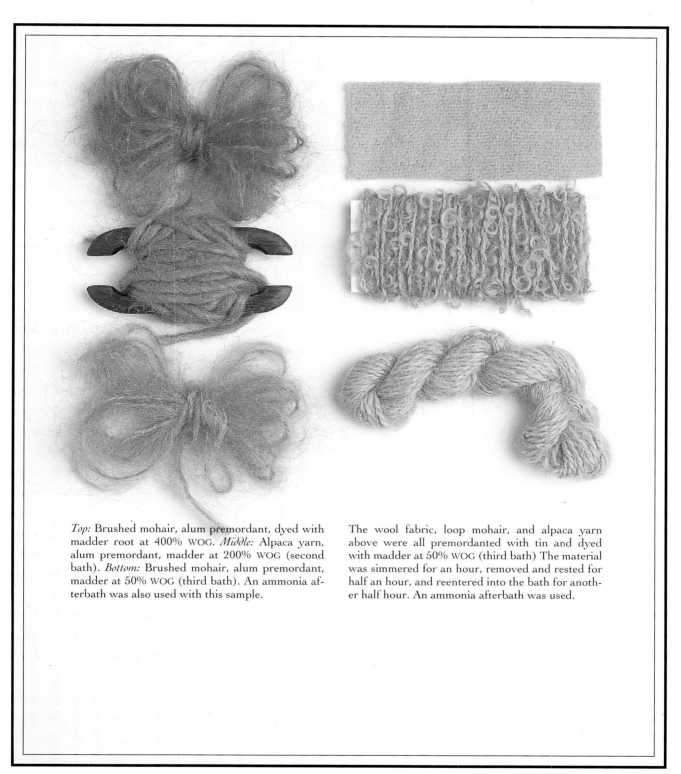

Top: Brushed mohair, alum premordant, dyed with madder root at 400% WOG. *Middle:* Alpaca yarn, alum premordant, madder at 200% WOG (second bath). *Bottom:* Brushed mohair, alum premordant, madder at 50% WOG (third bath). An ammonia afterbath was also used with this sample.

The wool fabric, loop mohair, and alpaca yarn above were all premordanted with tin and dyed with madder at 50% WOG (third bath) The material was simmered for an hour, removed and rested for half an hour, and reentered into the bath for another half hour. An ammonia afterbath was used.

RED SANDALWOOD (*Pterocarpus santalinus*) is a large tree native to India and Indonesia with compound leaves and yellow flowers like pea blossoms. The dyestuff, an insoluble powder, is produced from the heartwood. Used alone, it gives brownish reds, auburns, and burnt oranges, depending on the concentration and mordant used. The exhaust baths give soft pastel shades. Red sandalwood can also be used in combination with cutch or black walnut (see pages 96 and 99) to yield warm browns. It's a good dye for wool, mohair, and silk.

Dyeing with red sandalwood

Weigh the required amount of red sandalwood powder. Put it in a cup or jar with enough rubbing alcohol to make a thick paste and stir well. You may place the sandalwood loosely in a tightly knitted nylon stocking to avoid straining the dyebath later. Let the sandalwood/alcohol paste stand for 15 to 30 minutes, then put it in a dyepot of clean water, bring the water to a boil, and simmer for one hour. Make the dyebath just when you are ready to use it as prolonged soaking seems to dull the color.

Remove the stocking or strain the dyebath, and it is ready to use. Add the warmed, wetted fiber, bring the bath to a boil, and simmer for one hour.

RED SANDALWOOD Read the introductory material about this dyestuff carefully before using it; its color is not soluble in water and must be treated with alcohol in much the same way as brazilwood.

Silk yarn, alum premordant, red sandalwood at 200% WOG, ammonia afterbath.

Silk yarn, alum premordant, red sandalwood at 200% WOG.

Silk fabric, alum premordant, red sandalwood at 200% WOG, ammonia afterbath.

Silk-wool blend yarn, tin premordant, red sandalwood at 200% WOG.

BRAZILWOOD dye is produced from at least three tropical trees. The dyestuff available in chip form comes from *Haematoxylum brasiletta,* a tree closely related to logwood. Dyestuff in sawdust form comes from *Caesalpinia sappan,* a small tree (up to 20 feet tall) native to India and the Malay Peninsula, and *C. echinata,* a taller tree (up to 100 feet tall) found in Nicaragua, Colombia, and Venezuela. Both chips and sawdust are available from dye suppliers and give similar results.

Brazilwood produces bright crimsons and deep purples as well as pinks and corals on premordanted fibers. It gives better reds on cotton than cochineal does, and also dyes silk well. Brazilwood produces nice colors on wool or mohair but is not as fast as cochineal.

Dyeing with brazilwood

Sawdust yields its dye more readily than chips because it's in smaller pieces. If you buy chips, chop or grind them as fine as possible. Weigh out the brazilwood, put it in a small dish or pot, and add enough rubbing alcohol or alcohol mixed with water to cover. (You can use plain water, but I think the alcohol works better.)

Soak briefly to wet the wood, then spread it on a tray to sit for a few hours at room temperature. Exposure to moisture and air transforms a nearly colorless compound in the wood called brazilin into the active dye compound, brazilein.

Put the treated wood in a dyepot with enough water to cover the fiber you will be dyeing, bring to a boil, simmer for one hour, and strain. If you prefer, place the sawdust or chips loosely in a nylon stocking for the simmering. Remove the stocking before dyeing yarn, but leave it in if you're dyeing fleece and want some color variation; the wool that touches the dyestuff will come out darker than the rest. Simmer the premordanted fiber in the dyebath for an hour.

This recipe yields one strong dyebath and a few paler exhaust baths. The dye is exhausted much sooner than a cochineal dyebath of the same starting strength. After one or more baths, you can replenish the dyebath by putting the chips or sawdust back in and simmering for another hour. You might want to dry the wood and save it for later use, but it will yield less color the second time.

BRAZILWOOD Mohair often takes up dye more readily than other fibers do; the brushed mohair at bottom right on this page was dyed at half the strength of the silk fabric above it, yet shows a slightly stronger depth of shade. A little tin and washing soda in the dyebath give alum-mordanted fibers a bluish cast.

Right: Silk fabric, alum premordant, brazilwood at 100% WOG.

Below left: Brushed mohair, alum premordant, brazilwood at 100% WOG.

Below right: Brushed mohair, alum premordant, brazilwood at 50% WOG (second bath) with 0.5% tin and washing soda added to the dyebath.

BRAZILWOOD The first and second uses of a brazilwood dyebath (see previous page) exhaust most of the pigment, leaving only enough for pale pastels. But these pale shades are lovely, especially on silk, which gives them a pearly iridescence.

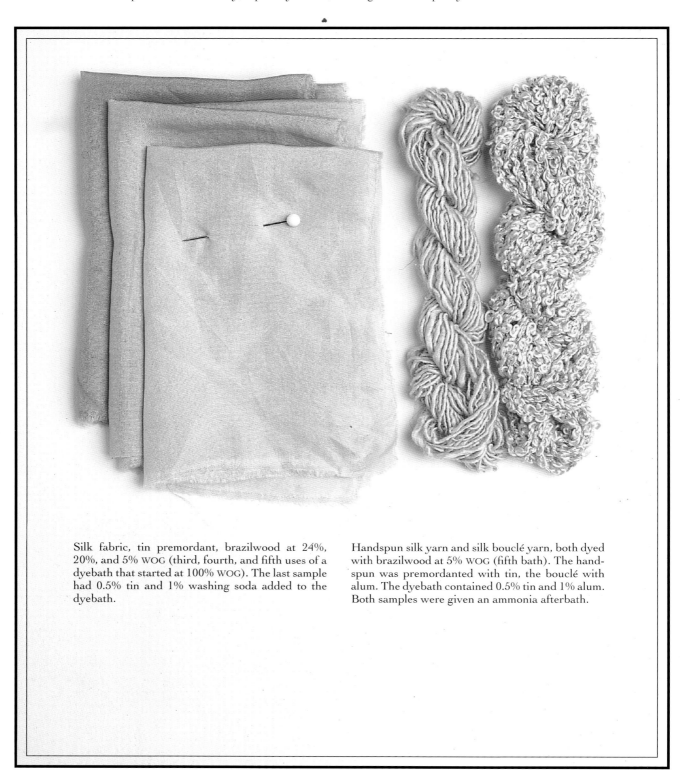

Silk fabric, tin premordant, brazilwood at 24%, 20%, and 5% WOG (third, fourth, and fifth uses of a dyebath that started at 100% WOG). The last sample had 0.5% tin and 1% washing soda added to the dyebath.

Handspun silk yarn and silk bouclé yarn, both dyed with brazilwood at 5% WOG (fifth bath). The handspun was premordanted with tin, the bouclé with alum. The dyebath contained 0.5% tin and 1% alum. Both samples were given an ammonia afterbath.

BRAZILWOOD As with other cotton samples in this book, these tend to show stronger color when premordanted with tara powder as well as alum.

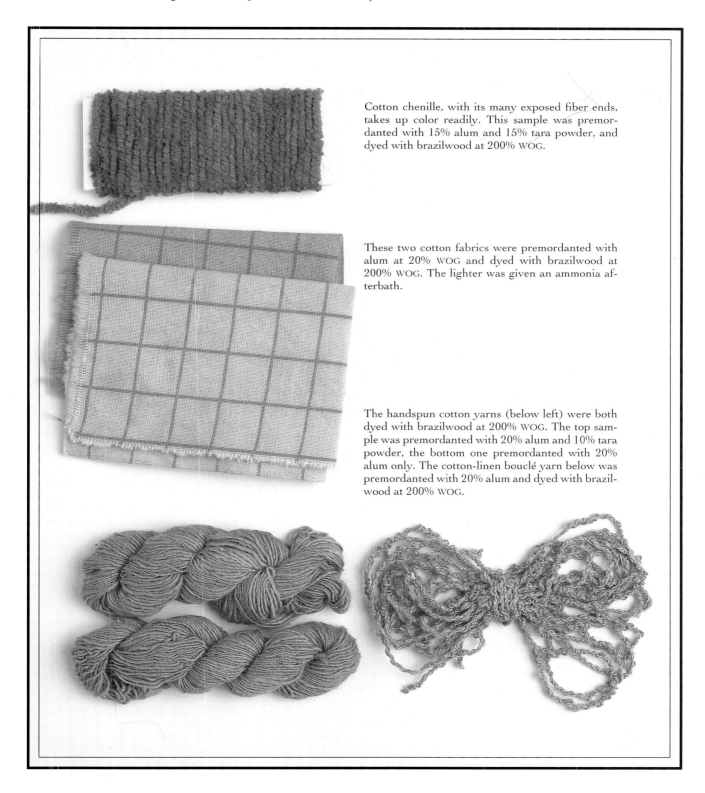

Cotton chenille, with its many exposed fiber ends, takes up color readily. This sample was premordanted with 15% alum and 15% tara powder, and dyed with brazilwood at 200% WOG.

These two cotton fabrics were premordanted with alum at 20% WOG and dyed with brazilwood at 200% WOG. The lighter was given an ammonia afterbath.

The handspun cotton yarns (below left) were both dyed with brazilwood at 200% WOG. The top sample was premordanted with 20% alum and 10% tara powder, the bottom one premordanted with 20% alum only. The cotton-linen bouclé yarn below was premordanted with 20% alum and dyed with brazilwood at 200% WOG.

COCHINEAL is the pulverized dried bodies of certain scale insects, *Dactylopius coccus*, which feed on prickly pear cacti. Though native to subtropical America, these insects are now cultivated in Peru, Mexico, the Canary Islands, and Australia. They are harvested by brushing them from the cactus plants into bags and then killed by immersion in hot water or by exposure to sunlight, steam, or oven heat. It takes 70,000 insects to make a pound of cochineal. Per pound, cochineal costs a lot more than other dyes, but a little goes a long way. It makes a wonderful range of colors, including the brightest reds you can find, the softest pinks, and a variety of other reds, pinks, purples, maroons, corals, and fuchsias. It mixes well and "warms" other dyes such as walnut, cutch, fustic, and marigold, but be careful not to add too much or it will overwhelm the other color. Cochineal works better on wool, mohair, and silk than on cotton. I use it with no mordant, with alum, and with tin.

Dyeing with cochineal

To extract the most color, you need to grind the cochineal into fine powder. Don't stop when it's gritty like sand or sugar; keep grinding until it's as fine as flour. I used to use an old manual coffee grinder when my son, David, was at home to crank it. Now, I use an electric coffee mill, but grinding cochineal wears out the blades so I have to replace them regularly. You might be tempted to skip the grinding and just put the cochineal in a nylon stocking, but I would advise against that. The cochineal lumps together, and the inside of the lump stays dry and therefore doesn't release any dye. I've tried soaking the cochineal for a few days instead of grinding it, but that treatment only releases a small percent of the potential color. So weigh out the amount of cochineal you need, start grinding, shake or stir, and grind once more.

Adding tartaric acid to the dyebath also helps increase the yield of color. Weigh out the specified amount of tartaric acid, and put it and the ground cochineal in a glass jar with enough cold water to cover. Stir well and let the mixture sit overnight.

The next day, fill a dyepot with enough water to cover the fiber to be dyed, bring it to a boil, stir in the cochineal/tartaric acid mixture, then boil for 15 minutes. A froth will rise to the surface. Before placing the fiber in the dye, strain or skim the solution to remove the small particles of ground cochineal caught in the froth. You can pour it through a strainer lined with a piece of fine-weave fabric such as old sheeting, but it's faster and easier simply to stir a tuft or handful of washed waste fleece through the dyebath. If that doesn't catch all the particles, repeat.

The addition of the tartaric acid makes the dyebath a bright orange-red (a cochineal bath without acid is dark wine red). Some of that brightness will be lost when you wash the dyed fiber, though. Using a tin mordant helps retain the bright scarlet red. According to the weight of the fiber you are dyeing, weigh out 0.5 percent or even 0.25 percent tin and dissolve it in a cup of water. Simmer the fiber in the cochineal/tartaric acid dyebath for 35 minutes, then remove it while you stir in the dissolved tin. Replace the fiber and simmer another five minutes. This method was discovered by the seventeenth-century Dutch chemist Cornelius Drebbel when he accidentally spilled a drop of tin solution into a cochineal bath.

Another method for obtaining bright scarlet, called "blooming the color", uses tin in the bath, or a separate tin afterbath.

Weigh out 0.5 percent tin and dissolve it in a pot of hot water. Transfer the dyed fiber into the hot tin solution, wait five minutes, then remove and rinse the fiber. Both methods give a good bright red on wool or mohair. (Silk is trickier, tending toward a bluish red unless you use a concentrated dyebath with tin and add a yellow dye such as fustic, as described below.)

To make purples from cochineal, I use an ammonia afterbath. Stir about 1/4 cup of household ammonia into a pail of hot water, and add the hot dyed fiber. Wool and mohair react dramatically and instantaneously, silk less so. This ammonia-induced color shift is permanent and stable, and makes lovely shades of purples with no harm to the fiber. (Some dyers use iron mordant to get purples from cochineal; I prefer not to because iron can seriously weaken fiber, especially silk.) For best results, always use hot water; the color change happens much more slowly if the ammonia solution is cold. If the ammonia from a partly used bottle is stale or weak, you may need to use more than 1/4 cup. If the solution is hot but the color doesn't shift, remove the fiber, stir in a little more ammonia, and try again. A dyebath that is not acid enough will produce a less dramatic color change, and the ammonia afterbath may give a washed-out look. If that happens, just add a little tartaric acid or a bit of tin to the dyebath—enough to change it from purplish back to orange. Rinse the fiber and put it back in the dyebath to brighten the color.

Mixing cochineal with marigolds or fustic—To mix cochineal with marigold for shades of orange, soak the marigold flowers overnight and prepare the cochineal and tartaric acid as outlined on page 82. The next day, brimg the dyebath to a boil and simmer it for an hour. Then strain the dyebath into a clean container, add the cochineal/tartaric acid mixture, and boil for 15 minutes. Skim or strain to re- move the cochineal residue, and you are ready to dye.

Cochineal mixed with fustic also gives orange. Fustic is a powder ground from the roots and wood of a tropical tree, *Chlorophora tinctoria*. It dissolves very easily and produces bright yellows. Weigh out the cochineal, tartaric acid, and fustic. Mix them in a jar of cold water and leave them to soak overnight. The next day, add the mixture to a dyepot of water, boil for 15 minutes and skim the residue. For a more or- ange color, use more fustic. Using less fustic gives a tomato red on silk. This bath is quite concentrated and can be reused six or seven times to give a se- ries of lighter shades.

COCHINEAL This is one of my favorite dyes—not only are the colors lovely, but they are so varied. The samples on this page are all kid mohair with no premordant. The labels under each sample indicate the percentage of dyestuff to WOG, and any additives to the bath or afterbaths. Simmering time is only 35 minutes.

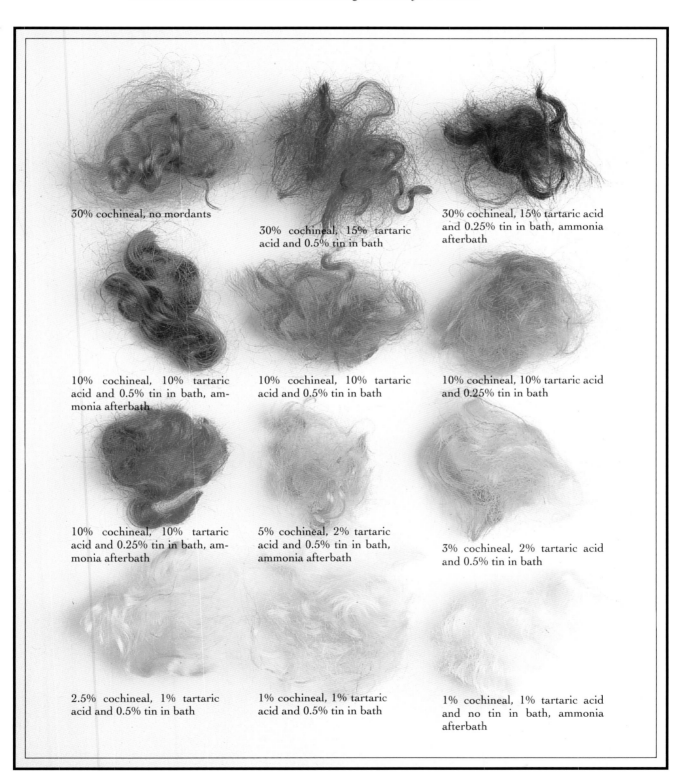

30% cochineal, no mordants

30% cochineal, 15% tartaric acid and 0.5% tin in bath

30% cochineal, 15% tartaric acid and 0.25% tin in bath, ammonia afterbath

10% cochineal, 10% tartaric acid and 0.5% tin in bath, ammonia afterbath

10% cochineal, 10% tartaric acid and 0.5% tin in bath

10% cochineal, 10% tartaric acid and 0.25% tin in bath

10% cochineal, 10% tartaric acid and 0.25% tin in bath, ammonia afterbath

5% cochineal, 2% tartaric acid and 0.5% tin in bath, ammonia afterbath

3% cochineal, 2% tartaric acid and 0.5% tin in bath

2.5% cochineal, 1% tartaric acid and 0.5% tin in bath

1% cochineal, 1% tartaric acid and 0.5% tin in bath

1% cochineal, 1% tartaric acid and no tin in bath, ammonia afterbath

COCHINEAL These samples, like those on the previous page, had no premordant. Note how dramatically the use of an ammonia afterbath, which changes pH, affects the colors of cochineal.

Above: Brushed mohair, no premordant, cochineal at 50% WOG. Handspun wool, no premordant, cochineal at 30% WOG. *Below:* Handspun wool, no premordant, cochineal at 3%, 2%, and 1% WOG with 1% tartaric acid and 0.5% tin in dyebath.

Above: Brushed mohair, no premordant, cochineal at 50% WOG, ammonia afterbath. Handspun wool, no premordant, cochineal at 30% WOG, ammonia afterbath.

Kid mohair (above) and wool fabric (left), no premordant, cochineal at 10% WOG, 10% tartaric acid and 0.5% tin in dyebath.

COCHINEAL These samples come from the second, third, fourth, and fifth uses of a cochineal dyebath that began at a strength of 30% WOG. Their dyestuff percentages are approximately 10%, 3%, 2%, and 1%. Color variations are also caused by mordants, additives, and afterbaths.

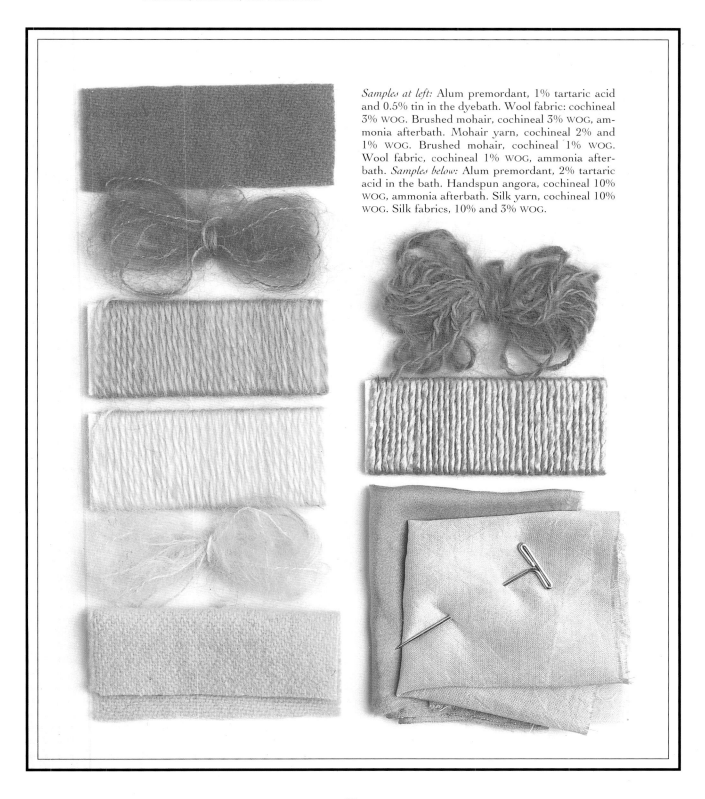

Samples at left: Alum premordant, 1% tartaric acid and 0.5% tin in the dyebath. Wool fabric: cochineal 3% WOG. Brushed mohair, cochineal 3% WOG, ammonia afterbath. Mohair yarn, cochineal 2% and 1% WOG. Brushed mohair, cochineal 1% WOG. Wool fabric, cochineal 1% WOG, ammonia afterbath. *Samples below:* Alum premordant, 2% tartaric acid in the bath. Handspun angora, cochineal 10% WOG, ammonia afterbath. Silk yarn, cochineal 10% WOG. Silk fabrics, 10% and 3% WOG.

COCHINEAL Higher ratios of cochineal to weight of goods, combined with a tin premordant, yield vivid crimson and cardinal reds. A small amount of tin in the dyebath, along with tartaric acid to keep the fibers from becoming harsh, further boosts the colors.

Above: Silk yarn, tin premordant, cochineal at 50% WOG, 0.5% tin in dyebath. *Below:* Mohair yarns, tin premordant, cochineal at 30% and 10% WOG respectively, 15% tartaric acid and 0.5% tin in dyebath. Second sample had ammonia afterbath. *Bottom:* Wool fabric, tin premordant, cochineal at 10% WOG 10% tartaric acid and 2.5% tin in dyebath.

Above: Alpaca yarn, tin premordant, cochineal at 30% WOG, 15% tartaric acid and 0.5% tin in dyebath. *Below:* Wool yarn, tin premordant, cochineal at 10% WOG, 10% tartaric acid and 2.5% tin in dyebath. Wool fabric, tin premordant, cochineal at 5% WOG, 10% tartaric acid and 2.5% tin in dyebath.

COCHINEAL Cochineal gives the same full range of colors on cotton as it does on the protein fibers, but I especially like the delicate pastels that result from lower percentages. The darker shades were premordanted with tara powder as well as alum.

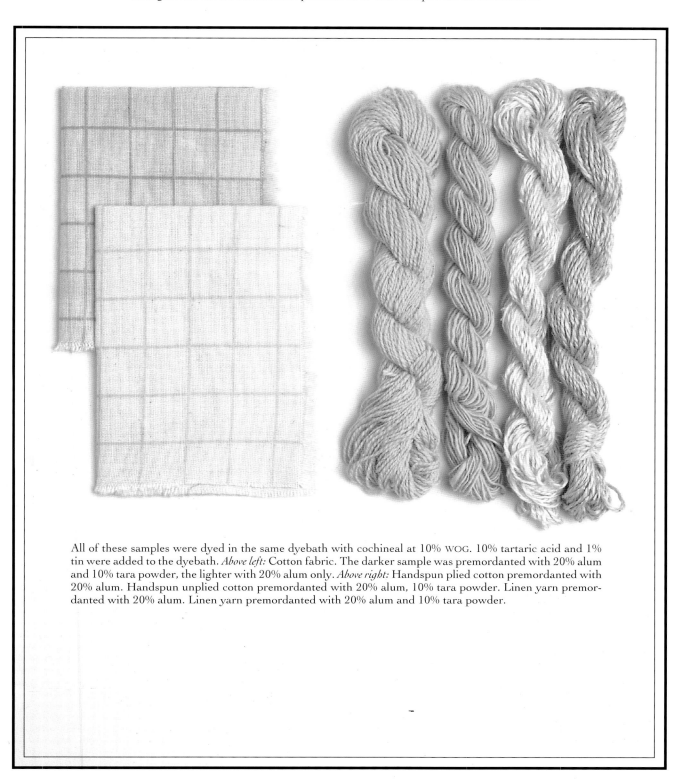

All of these samples were dyed in the same dyebath with cochineal at 10% WOG. 10% tartaric acid and 1% tin were added to the dyebath. *Above left:* Cotton fabric. The darker sample was premordanted with 20% alum and 10% tara powder, the lighter with 20% alum only. *Above right:* Handspun plied cotton premordanted with 20% alum. Handspun unplied cotton premordanted with 20% alum, 10% tara powder. Linen yarn premordanted with 20% alum. Linen yarn premordanted with 20% alum and 10% tara powder.

COCHINEAL & FUSTIC Fustic is a tropical dye that gives strong yellows with very little dyestuff. The samples below are all silk; the ones on the left were all pre-mordanted with alum, and those on the right with tin. Both mordants give similar shades; the color differences come from different relative percentages of the yellow and red dyestuffs.

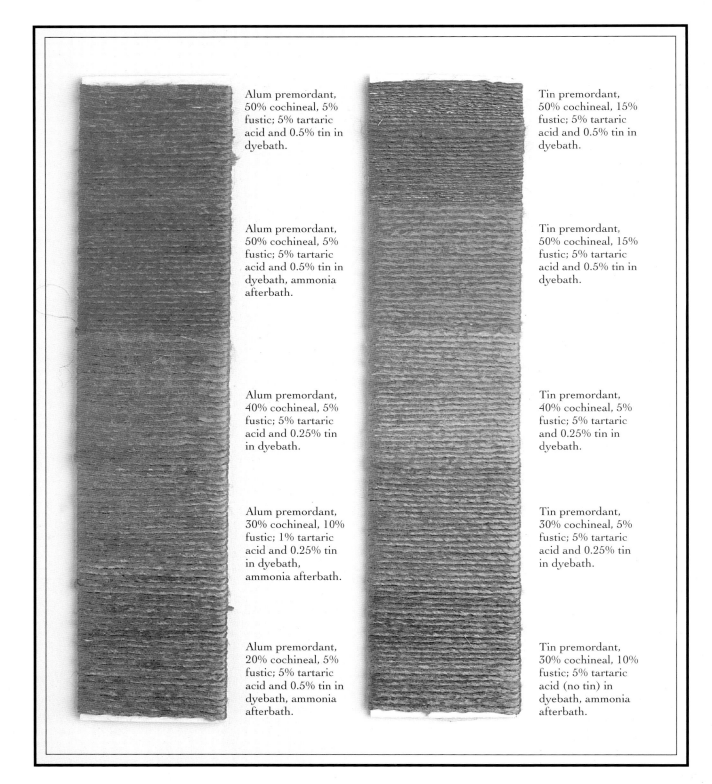

Alum premordant, 50% cochineal, 5% fustic; 5% tartaric acid and 0.5% tin in dyebath.

Tin premordant, 50% cochineal, 15% fustic; 5% tartaric acid and 0.5% tin in dyebath.

Alum premordant, 50% cochineal, 5% fustic; 5% tartaric acid and 0.5% tin in dyebath, ammonia afterbath.

Tin premordant, 50% cochineal, 15% fustic; 5% tartaric acid and 0.5% tin in dyebath.

Alum premordant, 40% cochineal, 5% fustic; 5% tartaric acid and 0.25% tin in dyebath.

Tin premordant, 40% cochineal, 5% fustic; 5% tartaric and 0.25% tin in dyebath.

Alum premordant, 30% cochineal, 10% fustic; 1% tartaric acid and 0.25% tin in dyebath, ammonia afterbath.

Tin premordant, 30% cochineal, 5% fustic; 5% tartaric acid and 0.25% tin in dyebath.

Alum premordant, 20% cochineal, 5% fustic; 5% tartaric acid and 0.5% tin in dyebath, ammonia afterbath.

Tin premordant, 30% cochineal, 10% fustic; 5% tartaric acid (no tin) in dyebath, ammonia afterbath.

COCHINEAL & MARIGOLD As with cochineal and fustic, it's the relative strengths of the two dyestuffs that most affect hue. Marigolds require a higher percentages of dye material to weight of goods than fustic to shift the strong reds of cochineal toward orange.

All the samples above were dyed in the same bath with cochineal at 20% WOG and marigold at 200% WOG. The dyebath also contained 10% tartaric acid. The three sample on the left were premordanted with alum, and those on the right with tin. The slightly bluer sample, third from left, is a silk-wool blend, whereas the other samples are pure silk. The mohair yarn at right was premordanted with tin and dyed with 2% cochineal and 200% marigold with 10% tartaric acid in the dyebath.

CUTCH (*Acacia catechu*) is a small, thorny tree native to tropical India and Burma. The dyestuff is a gummy resin extracted by boiling chips of the heartwood in water. The extract is formed into rough blocks and wrapped in large leaves to dry; it is then broken into smaller chunks. The form sold to dyers looks like shiny brown stones.

Cutch extract produces beautiful rich browns and rusts, and the colors are fast even without mordant. Cutch is especially lovely on silk but also works well on cotton and wool. It can be combined with other dyes. Adding some madder or sandalwood to a cutch dyebath makes warmer, reddish browns. Combining cutch with Saxon blue indigo gives forest greens.

Dyeing with cutch

The main challenge in dyeing with cutch is dissolving the extract. Weigh the required amount of cutch, then use one of the following methods. If you're in a hurry, put the cutch in a jar of hot water and stir well. When the water starts to cool, pour it into the dyepot. Refill the jar with more hot water and stir again, wait a bit, then pour that into the dyepot. Repeat until all the cutch has dissolved. Don't try heating undissolved cutch in the dyepot unless you're willing to stir continuously; otherwise it will stick to the bottom and burn onto your pot.

The slower but easier way to dissolve cutch is simply to soak it in a dyepot of cold water for 24 hours. Stir from time to time.

As soon as it is completely dissolved, cutch is ready to use. Add the weighed and wetted fiber, bring the dyebath to a boil, and simmer for one hour, then remove from the heat and let the fiber soak in the cooling dyebath for another hour or longer. The additional soaking time produces darker colors and improves the dye's fastness.

CUTCH With no mordant, cutch dyes protein fibers a medium warm tan. Mordants deepen and enrich the colors as shown below. The darker samples resulted from a ratio of four times as much cutch as fiber by weight. The lighter samples were dyed in the second bath, when the amount of dyestuff had reduced to about two and a half times the weight of goods. Subsequent baths would continue to produce good color, as you can see from the cotton samples on the next page.

Wool fabric, tin premordant, cutch at 400% WOG.

Silk loop yarn, alum premordant, cutch at 400% WOG.

Silk yarn, tin premordant, cutch at 400% WOG, ammonia afterbath.

Silk yarn, cutch at 250% WOG (second bath).

Silk fabrics, both alum premordant, cutch at 400% and 250% WOG (first and second baths).

CUTCH All the samples on this page were dyed with cutch at 50% WOG. The color variations are caused by different fibers and the use of tara powder, which is rich in tannic acid, in addition to alum.

Handspun cotton, premordanted with 20% alum, dyed with cutch at 50% WOG. The top sample is natural white cotton, the other is natural brown cotton (a light tan).

Cotton chenille, premordanted with 15% alum and 15% tara powder. Dyed with cutch at 50% WOG.

Cotton and linen bouclé yarn (one strand of each plied together), premordanted with 20% alum and 10% tara powder, dyed with cutch at 50% WOG.

BLACK WALNUT (*Juglans nigra*) is a deciduous tree native to eastern North America. It grows 70 to 100 feet tall and 2 to 3 feet in diameter and is valued for its attractive, dark-colored heartwood lumber as well as for its sweet, oily nuts. The woody-shelled nuts are enclosed in yellowish green hulls that are as thick as orange or grapefruit rinds. The hulls provide rich brown and tan dyes. Walnut leaves are also used sometimes; they produce lighter brown dyes.

The nuts mature and drop in fall. Because walnuts stain everything, wear old clothes and rubber gloves when you gather or handle them.* Only the hulls are needed for dyeing, but removing them is such a messy job that I usually use the whole nuts. You can use walnuts for dyeing while the hulls are still fresh and green or spread them out to dry for later use. I gather walnuts in the fall, store them outside in plastic bags over the winter; and use them for dyeing the following spring and summer.

Walnut hulls give good browns and beiges on wool, mohair, silk, and cotton with no mordant, but the colors are faster if mordants are used. Walnut mixes well with other dyes to produce a wider range of colors.

Dyeing with walnuts

The following recipes call for whole dried nuts. If you want to use fresh nuts, you'll need to use five times the amounts called for. Weigh out the nuts and put them in a dyepot full of water to soak overnight. If you put them inside a net bag it's easier to remove them later. The next day, bring the water to a vigorous boil and boil hard, covered, for at least 90 minutes. Strain the dyebath through a piece of tightly woven cloth into another pot. Straining is messy but important, as any bits of hull that remain in the dyebath will make dark spots on the fiber. Clean the dyepot thoroughly, also, removing all stains. Add the warmed, wetted fiber to the dyebath, bring it to a boil, and keep at a gentle boil for 90 minutes (not just 60 minutes, as for other dyes). Remove the dyed fiber and rinse well.

---

*One year, I spent a day gathering walnuts with my bare hands. We were invited to a party that night, but my hands looked so terrible that I hesitated to go. I washed and scrubbed but none of the color came off. Finally I put my hands in undiluted bleach. The dirty look disappeared, but then I smelled like I had been cleaning all day. The moral of this story is, "When working with walnuts, wear gloves."

Using black walnuts with red sandal-wood—This recipe, which calls for a single dyebath, produces a warm reddish brown. I use it to dye mohair or wool for wonderful "redhead" doll hair. Weigh out the required amount of walnuts. Also weigh the required amount of red sandalwood sawdust or powder, which had been soaked in alcohol (see page 76), and place it loosely in a nylon stocking. Put dyestuffs in a dyepot of water and soak overnight. The next day, bring the bath to a vigorous boil and boil, covered, for 90 minutes. Strain the dyebath through a piece of tightly woven cloth, and it will be ready to use. Add the warmed, wetted fiber, heat to boiling, and keep at a gentle boil for 90 minutes.

Using black walnuts with fustic—This combination also makes very realistic-looking doll hair. The color can be altered by adding more or less fustic. Weigh out the required amount of walnuts and soak them overnight in a pot of water. The next day, bring the water to a boil and boil, covered, for 90 minutes, then strain the dyebath through a piece of tightly woven cloth. Add the required amount of fustic powder and stir well to dissolve it. The dyebath is then ready to use. This dye combination works without a mordant, a real advantage when dyeing fleece. Handling fleece as little as possible keeps the locks in shape, but the fleece must be washed very clean before dyeing so that the doll hair will be evenly colored.

BLACK WALNUT Black walnut dye needs no mordant; the tannic acid in the hulls acts as one. But as noted in the introduction, alum or tin premordants make black walnut's colors more fast; they also shift the color slightly toward yellow or red, as you can see on the following page. Black walnut yields more color with longer simmering time; an hour and a half is recommended.

Brushed mohair, no mordant. Black walnut at 1000% WOG, or ten times as much dyestuff as fiber by weight. The darker sample on the right had an ammonia afterbath.

Handspun wool yarns, no mordant, black walnut at 500% and 150% WOG respectively (second and third dyebaths).

Unspun kid mohair, no mordant, black walnut at 15% WOG (seventh dyebath).

BLACK WALNUT Remember that the ratios in these recipes are based on dried nuts.
If you are using fresh nuts, five times as many are needed to get comparable colors.

The samples above were all premordanted with alum. *From the top:* Wool fabric, 1000% WOG (first dyebath). Wool fabric, 500% WOG (second bath). Alpaca yarn, 100% WOG (fourth bath). Mohair yarn, 35% WOG (sixth bath).

The samples in this column are similar in sequence to the ones at left, but with a tin premordant. *From the top:* Handspun wool yarn, 1000% WOG (first bath). Wool yarn, 500% WOG (second bath). Alpaca yarn, 150% WOG (third bath). Handspun silk-wool yarn, 15% WOG (seventh bath).

BLACK WALNUT & RED SANDALWOOD Red sandalwood combined with black walnut gives wonderful russet and auburn hues. Remember that the sandalwood must be soaked in alcohol in order for its color to be released into the dyebath (see page 76). All the samples on this page used red sandalwood at 100% and black walnut at 50% WOG.

Above left: Wool fabric, alum premordant. The center sample had an ammonia afterbath. *Below left:* Brushed mohair, alum premordant. The bottom sample had an ammonia afterbath. *Above:* Alpaca yarn, tin premordant. The lower sample had an ammonia afterbath. *Below:* Wool fabric, tin premordant. In this case, the darker sample had an ammonia afterbath.

SUMACS are shrubs or small trees that grow wild in waste areas, old fields, and at edges of woods and pastures. Three species are common throughout eastern North America: smooth sumac (*Rhus glabra*), staghorn sumac (*R. typhina*), and shining sumac *R. copallina*). They are sometimes planted as ornamentals in the western states. All have compound leaves that turn bright red in fall, and thick branches topped with cucumber-sized clusters of sticky, velvety fruits that ripen red in fall and last through the winter. Boiling these fruits makes a fragrant pot of red liquid, but unfortunately the red doesn't transfer to the fibers, so the resulting color is just beige. Adding iron mordant transforms it into a warm gray.

Dyeing with sumac

Gather the required weight of sumac fruits (you can use the whole cluster and don't need to strip the berries from their stalks) and soak them overnight in a pot of clean water. The next day, bring the water to a boil, simmer for one hour, and strain. Add the warmed, wetted fiber and simmer for one hour to get beige. To get a warm gray, simmer the fiber for one hour, then remove it while you add iron mordant (use 2 or 3 percent of the weight of the fiber) to the dyebath and stir well. Return the fiber to the dyebath and simmer for 15 minutes longer.

SUMAC It takes only a small amount of iron mordant to transform the golden-beige color that sumac berries give on their own to a rich, warm gray.

Above: Brushed mohair, tin premordant, sumac berries at 800% WOG. *Above right:* The percentage of sumac berries to WOG has been reduced to 400, but 3% iron has been added to the dyebath after the tin-mordanted silk fabric has simmered for an hour. *Center right:* Silk yarn, alum premordant, sumac berries at 400% WOG, with 3% iron added to the bath after simmering an hour. *Bottom right:* The same recipe as for the silk yarn above was used for this handspun silk-wool blend yarn.

ALKANET (*Alkanna tinctoria*) is a low-growing perennial with pretty blue flowers. Native to southern Europe, it is cultivated in France for its thick, papery-barked roots, which are used for dyeing. An alkanet dyebath smells absolutely dreadful but gives wonderful, unusual colors. The color of the dyebath turns pinkish in acid conditions and grayish blue in alkaline ones. Mordants also affect the color: tin gives a grayish pink whereas alum gives soft gray-blues and gray-greens.

Dyeing with alkanet

Weigh out the required amount of roots and cut them into small pieces with a knife or pruning shears. Put the pieces in a glass or plastic cup, cover them with rubbing alcohol, and let them stand for one hour or so. Don't let them soak overnight, or some of the color will be lost. Fill a dyepot with warm water, add the alkanet/alcohol mixture, bring the bath to a boil, and boil for an hour. Strain the liquid into another pot; it is now ready to use.

Add the premordanted, warmed, wetted fiber. Bring to a boil and simmer for one hour.

ALKANET Photographic and printing processes don't do justice to the dark, mysterious grays of alkanet. Explore smaller percentages of dyestuff as well as pH modification with vinegar or ammonia afterbaths.

Wool fabric, wool yarn, and handspun angora yarn, all with alum premordant and dyed with alkanet at 400% WOG.

Below left: Loop mohair, alum premordant (left) and tin (right), dyed with alkanet at 400% WOG. The tin imparts a faint pink cast to the yarn. *Below:* Alpaca and brushed mohair, both premordanted with tin and dyed with alkanet at 200% WOG.

L O G W O O D

LOGWOOD (*Haematoxylum campechianum*) is a small, thorny tree native to the Yucatan Peninsula and West Indies. It grows to 25 feet tall, and it has an odd trunk that looks like a bunch of sticks which have grown together. The heartwood, the part used for dyeing, is sold both as sawdust and as chips.

Logwood produces many shades of pinks, blues, maroons, and purples, as well as a few grayish greens, depending on the mordants used. Tin gives a range from pink to purple or maroon, alum gives blues or bluish grays, and alum with copper gives dark blues. Strong concentrations of logwood yield surprising brownish purple shades, especially on silk. Although I try to use as little mordant as possible, mordanting is essential to make logwood colors fast. Even when mordants are used, the colors are not as lightfast as many other dyes. Logwood may be used on wool, mohair, silk, and cotton.

Dyeing with logwood

Weigh out the required amount of logwood sawdust or chips (if using chips, chop them as finely as possible) and put it in a nylon stocking. Soak in a dyepot of cold water for at least one hour, or preferably overnight. At the end of the soaking period, the dyebath should be a bright purplish red. If it is brownish red, the solution is too acidic. Add washing soda, a little at a time (start with a teaspoonful) until the dyebath turns bright purplish red. Bring it to a boil and simmer for one hour, then remove the stocking of dyestuff. Add the premordanted fiber and simmer for an hour.

Using logwood with goldenrod or marigold—This is one of my favorite dye combinations. It makes wonderful brassy greens and needs only a little mordant to achieve good fastness. Strong concentrations of both dyes (i.e., 50% logwood and 200% yellow) makes a deep near-black on wool. The process consists of two steps: first dyeing the fiber blue with logwood, then topdyeing with goldenrod.

Chop and weigh the goldenrod or marigold, and soak it in water overnight. The next day, bring the water to a boil and simmer it for one hour. Strain the dyebath into another pot.

Rather than using a new logwood dyebath, which is likely to be too strong, it's better to use an exhaust bath—a dyebath that's already been used two or three times. Use yarn that has been premordanted with alum, or, if you want to dye fleece, weigh out copper sulfate equal to 2 percent of the fiber weight and add it to the dyepot, stirring well. Put the yarn or fleece into the logwood dyebath, bring to a boil, and simmer for one hour. This will give a basic blue, and the final green will depend on the intensity of this blue.

Remove the fiber and spin to extract any excess blue dye, then put it in the yellow dyebath and simmer for one hour. This gives a very fast green dye that also smells good.

Any of the other yellow dyes described in this book can be used as well. An example of logwood overdyed with Osage orange is shown on page 109.

Using logwood with Saxon blue indigo—This gives a dark blue that is much faster than logwood used alone. It's also a cheaper alternative to mixing cochineal with Saxon blue. Weigh out the required amount of logwood sawdust or chips (if using chips, chop them as fine as possible) and put it in a nylon stocking. Soak in a dyepot of cold water for at least one hour, or preferably overnight. At the end of the soaking period, the dyebath should be a bright purplish red. If it is brownish red, the solution is too acidic. Add washing soda, a little at a time (start with a teaspoonful) until the dyebath turns bright purplish red. Bring it to a boil and simmer for one hour, then remove the stocking of dyestuff. Add fiber premordanted with alum and simmer for an hour. Remove the fiber from the logwood dyebath and spin to remove excess dye.

Fill a separate pot with clean hot water and add the required amount of Saxon blue solution. Put in the fiber and simmer for 30 minutes. The color will not change greatly, but the fastness will be much improved.

LOGWOOD The samples on this page show clearly how logwood colors are affected by the percentage of dyestuff used. These samples came from successive immersions in the same dyebath; the last, palest colors exhausted the bath. These effects are most pronounced on silk—the browns that result from higher percentages seem to happen only on this fiber.

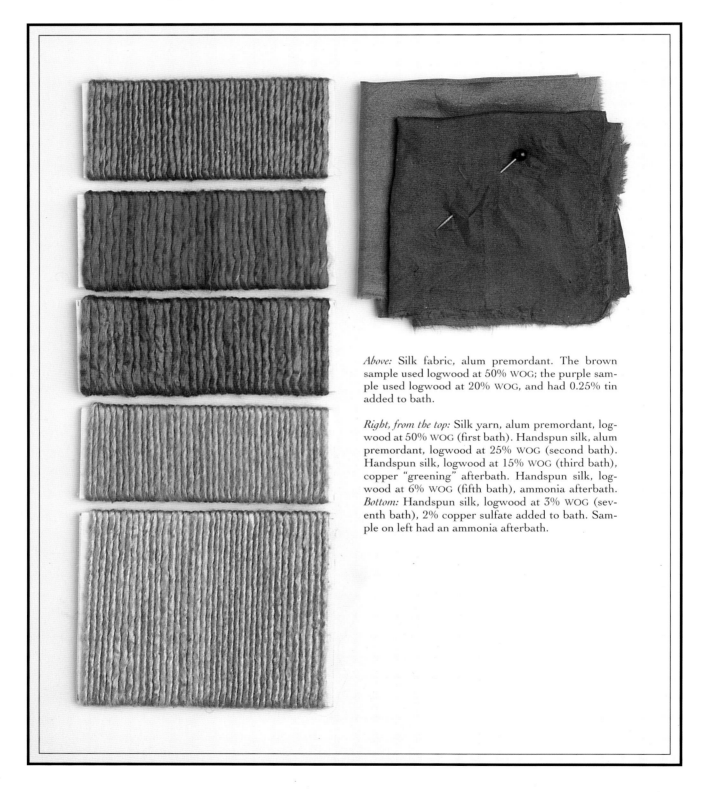

Above: Silk fabric, alum premordant. The brown sample used logwood at 50% WOG; the purple sample used logwood at 20% WOG, and had 0.25% tin added to bath.

Right, from the top: Silk yarn, alum premordant, logwood at 50% WOG (first bath). Handspun silk, alum premordant, logwood at 25% WOG (second bath). Handspun silk, logwood at 15% WOG (third bath), copper "greening" afterbath. Handspun silk, logwood at 6% WOG (fifth bath), ammonia afterbath. *Bottom:* Handspun silk, logwood at 3% WOG (seventh bath), 2% copper sulfate added to bath. Sample on left had an ammonia afterbath.

LOGWOOD Tin premordants bring out redder hues. As with the samples premordanted with alum, higher percentages of dyestuff result in surprising reddish-brown shades.

Above: Handspun silk, tin premordant, logwood at 50% WOG (left) and 20% WOG (right). *Below:* Mohair yarn (left) and wool yarn (right), tin premordant, logwood at 10% WOG. The mohair yarn had a copper "greening" afterbath.

Above: Silk fabric, tin premordant, dyed successively. The brown sample came from the first use of the bath at a ratio of 50% logwood to WOG; the rose sample was from the sixth bath at a ratio of 10% logwood to WOG; and the gray sample was from the seventh bath at a ratio of 5% logwood to WOG, with the addition of 0.25% copper to the bath.

LOGWOOD The addition of tara powder, which is rich in tannic acid, to alum in mordanting cotton sometimes makes a dramatic difference in the resulting color. The darker, redder shades below use higher percentages of tara powder. All samples were dyed with only 20% of dyestuff to the weight of goods.

Above: Handspun cotton yarns, premordanted with 20% alum and dyed with logwood at 20% WOG. The lighter sample had an ammonia afterbath.

Left, from the top: Handspun cotton premordanted with 20% alum and 10% tara powder, dyed with logwood at 20% WOG. Cotton/linen blend yarn dyed with logwood at 20% WOG. The darker sample on the left was premordanted with 15% alum and 15% tara powder; the lighter purple sample on the right was premordanted with 20% alum and 10% tara powder. Cotton chenille, premordanted with 15% alum and 15% tara powder, dyed with logwood at 20% WOG. Cotton fabric, dyed with logwood at 20% WOG. The darker sample on the left was premordanted with 15% alum and 15% tara powder; the lighter sample was premordanted with 20% alum and 10% tara powder.

LOGWOOD & YELLOWS A strong logwood dyebath will tend to overwhelm any yellow dye, even the most potent. The samples shown here use only 10 or 15% of logwood to weight of goods, and much higher percentages of yellow dyestuff in the second dyebaths.

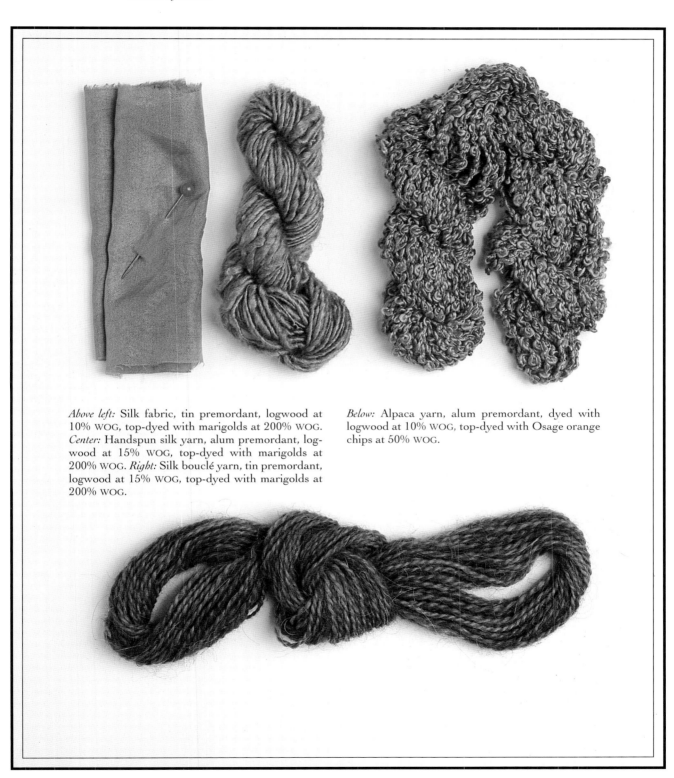

Above left: Silk fabric, tin premordant, logwood at 10% WOG, top-dyed with marigolds at 200% WOG. *Center:* Handspun silk yarn, alum premordant, logwood at 15% WOG, top-dyed with marigolds at 200% WOG. *Right:* Silk bouclé yarn, tin premordant, logwood at 15% WOG, top-dyed with marigolds at 200% WOG.

Below: Alpaca yarn, alum premordant, dyed with logwood at 10% WOG, top-dyed with Osage orange chips at 50% WOG.

ORCHIL or archil (*Roccella tinctoria*) is a lichen found throughout Canada except on the prairies and in the United States on the East Coast, around the Great Lakes, and in the Appalachians and mountain regions of the West excluding Nevada. It usually grows on rocks just above the waterline or in hard-to-reach places such as steep, moist cliffs. It forms shallow cups, about 3 inches wide, that are attached to the rock at one central point on the bottom. When dry, the lichen is quite stiff, with a soft gray velvety upper surface and black-brown "hairs" on the bottom.

It's easiest to collect the lichen when it is wet. Then the texture is soft and rubbery, and the color is a slimy green. Never pick more than a fraction of the lichen in one location. It grows very slowly, and you need only a little to dye with. If you let the lichen dry until it is crisp, you can store it for future use.

Orchil produces beautiful pinks and fuchsia on wool, mohair, and silk, but definitely needs a mordant for fastness so it's not suitable for dyeing fleeces. The colors are lovely, but because it grows so slowly, I'm reluctant to use very much orchil for dyeing, and often choose cochineal instead.

Dyeing with orchil

You'll need to plan in advance before dyeing with orchil—it takes days or weeks to extract the dye. Weigh out 100 grams of dry lichen, enough to dye several hundred grams of fiber, and crumble it into bits. Place the lichen in a glass jar with 1 cup of ammonia and 2 cups of water and stir well. Cover the jar to keep the fumes inside and set it in a safe, warm place. Twice daily for at least 10 days, stir vigorously to mix air into the solution. At this point, the liquid will be a rich, dark reddish purple. You can use it now, but waiting another two weeks or more will extract even more color from the lichen. It won't go bad even if you leave it soaking for a few months. When you are ready to dye, strain the liquid into another container. You can add more ammonia and water to the lichen to extract more dye from it.

Weigh out the required amount of the liquid and add it to a dyepot full of water. Add the warmed, wetted, premordanted fiber, bring the water to a boil, and simmer for an hour.

ORCHIL LICHEN When boiled in water as is usual with most natural dyes, orchil lichens give disappointing grays at best. A lengthy soaking in ammonia is necessary to release their intense purples. Note that percentages of dyestuff to weight of goods is figured on the weight of the ammonia solution, not on the weight of the lichen itself.

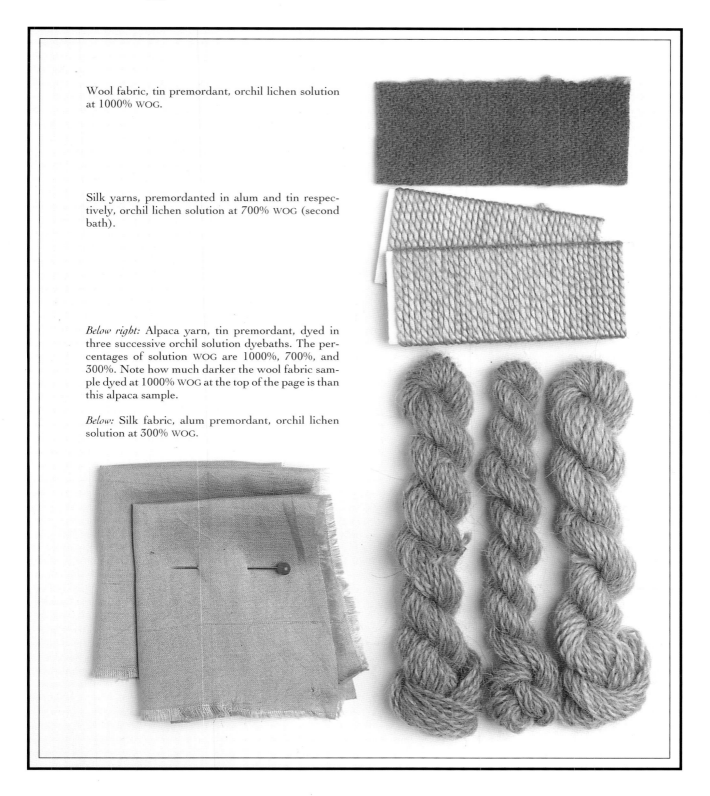

Wool fabric, tin premordant, orchil lichen solution at 1000% WOG.

Silk yarns, premordanted in alum and tin respectively, orchil lichen solution at 700% WOG (second bath).

Below right: Alpaca yarn, tin premordant, dyed in three successive orchil solution dyebaths. The percentages of solution WOG are 1000%, 700%, and 300%. Note how much darker the wool fabric sample dyed at 1000% WOG at the top of the page is than this alpaca sample.

Below: Silk fabric, alum premordant, orchil lichen solution at 300% WOG.

INDIGO is an ancient dyestuff which has been produced since at least 2500 B.C. from many different kinds of plants. Two of the most important are *Indigofera tinctoria*, a small shrubby plant native to the Old World tropics, and *I. suffruticosa*, a similar species native to the New World. Both have compound leaves with many small leaflets. Extracting the dyestuff from these leaves requires several steps. First, the plants are cut and steeped in warm water. This releases indoxyl, a colorless precursor to the indigo dye. Adding oxygen (by vigorously stirring the solution) converts the indoxyl into the blue indigo pigment, which can then be concentrated into blocks or chunks and dried. You can buy these chunks of natural indigo, which look like blue stones, or indigo that has been crushed into a fine powder. The powdered form is much easier to use.

Indigo produces a wide variety of blues ranging from pale baby blue to dark, deep blackish blue. It's a good dye for the whole gamut of natural fibers, including wool, mohair, silk, cotton, and flax. No mordant is required, though I usually use a mordant, especially if I plan to overdye the fiber or combine another dyestuff with the indigo.

Traditionally, indigo was used in a process called vat dyeing. Most natural dye books tell how to set up and use an indigo vat. I prefer to use indigo in a form called Saxon blue, which is prepared from an old industrial recipe used in eighteenth-century Europe. Saxon blue is a concentrated solution of indigo powder mixed with sulfuric acid and calcium carbonate. It's very easy to use, and it's easily mixed with other dyes to get a whole range of greens and purples. Used alone, Saxon blue colors fade somewhat upon exposure to light, but in combination with other dyestuffs, the resulting colors are quite fast.

Preparing and using the Saxon blue indigo solution

You can buy bottles of Saxon blue solution that's ready to use, or you can prepare it yourself from powdered indigo, powdered calcium carbonate, and concentrated sulfuric acid. Indigo is available from any mail-order dye supplier and many local spinning and weaving shops. Calcium carbonate is the same as limestone or chalk; you can get ground limestone at a garden center, or powdered chalk from a pharmacist. It's harder to buy a small amount of concentrated sulfuric acid. If you can't order it through a pharmacist, check the Yellow Pages under "Chemicals".

You must be very careful when handling sulfuric acid. It is very corrosive, and the fumes are noxious. Work outdoors or in an open, well-ventilated garage. Wear an industrial face mask, safety glasses, rubber boots and gloves, and a heavy-duty rubber or plastic apron. (Check the Yellow Pages under "Safety Equipment and Clothing" or "Laboratory Equipment and Supplies", or order by mail from Lab Safety Supply, Inc., PO Box 1368, Janesville, WI 53547.)

Having taken these safety precautions, weigh out 14 grams of indigo and 7 grams of calcium carbonate, and put them in a large wide-mouthed glass jar. Weigh 90 grams of 98 percent sulfuric acid in a glass beaker with a pour spout. Very slowly and carefully, pour one-half of the acid into the jar, stirring with a glass stirring rod. Stay calm. The mixture in the jar will get very hot and foam furiously. Keep stirring. Slowly add the rest of the sulfuric acid, and continue stirring until the solution settles down. Cover the jar with a sheet of plastic wrap (the acid would corrode an unprotected metal lid) and put it in a safe place, out of reach of children or pets. Stir the solution daily for 10 to 14 days. Then it will be ready to use. The indigo should be completely dissolved, and the calcium carbonate will have neutralized the sulfuric acid so that the solution is no longer dangerous to handle. At this point, you can transfer the solution to a smaller jar for storage. It will last almost indefinitely.

I used to measure out the solution with an eye dropper, but that method wasn't accurate enough to give consistent results. Now, I measure the Saxon blue by weight as I do mordants. Because it is strong, only small amounts are needed; further, the turquoise and teal shades that can be obtained from small percentages of dyestuff are lovely, and combine well with other dyes. That makes accurate measuring all the more important.

Dyeing with Saxon blue—Fill a dyepot with clean water and add the amount of Saxon blue solution specified in the recipe. Put in the warmed, wetted fiber, bring the water to a boil, and simmer for at least 30 minutes. When you remove the dyed fiber, the water should be almost clear.

Using Saxon blue indigo with cochineal—The combination of indigo and cochineal gives a wonderful range of colors from deep purple and dark ultramarine blue to lilacs, lavenders, and soft pinkish gray. With this combination, I always start with cochineal and "set" the red or pink color on the fiber, then add the indigo later. Starting with indigo gives duller colors.

Weigh out the required amounts of finely ground cochineal and tartaric acid, stir them into a small jar of cold water, and let them stand overnight. The next day, add the contents of the jar to a dyepot of clean water, bring the water to a boil, and boil for 15 minutes. Strain or skim the dyebath to remove the bits of cochineal. Enter the warmed, wetted fiber and simmer, according to the time specified in the recipe. Lift the fiber from the dyebath, add the required amount of Saxon blue solution, then put the fiber back in and simmer at least 30 minutes.

The combination of cochineal/tartaric acid and Saxon blue makes an acid dyebath. Dipping the dyed fiber in an ammonia afterbath will cause a striking color shift. Add 1/4 cup household ammonia to a pail of hot water and soak the dyed fiber in it for about five minutes to produce rich blues and purples.

Adding a small amount of tin—about 0.5 percent of the weight of the fiber—to the mixed cochineal/Saxon blue dyebath will intensify and brighten the colors. These may also be dipped in an ammonia afterbath.

Using Saxon blue indigo with marigolds—The Saxon blue dye solution can be mixed right into a dyebath made from marigolds or other "local yellow" dyes to create beautiful greens. First, prepare the yellow dyebath. When using marigolds, I pick only the lightest yellow flowers—no leaves. Crush and bruise the flowers, weigh out enough for the recipe, and put them in a pot, covered with water, to soak overnight. The next day, bring the water to a boil and simmer one hour, then strain the dyebath into a clean pot. Add the prepared yarn or fiber and simmer for 30 minutes to "set" the yellow color. Then remove the fiber, add the required amount of Saxon blue solution, and stir. Return the fiber to the dyepot and simmer for another 30 minutes.

Using Saxon blue indigo with goldenrod—For this combination, I like to pick goldenrod early in the season when the tops are still greenish and use both the leaves and the flower buds. Chop and weigh the flower stalks and put them in a pot, covered with water, to soak overnight. The next day, bring the water to a boil and simmer one hour, then strain the dyebath into a clean pot. Add the prepared fiber and simmer for 30 minutes to "set" the yellow color. Then remove the fiber, add the required amount of Saxon blue solution, and stir. Return the fiber to the dyepot and simmer for another 30 minutes.

Using Saxon blue indigo with Osage orange—Osage orange (*Maclura pomifera*) is a spiny tree native to Arkansas and Texas but planted throughout the midwestern and northeastern states (see page 65). Its wood is a bright golden yellow and makes a very clear lemon yellow dye. The combination of Osage orange and indigo gives bright but delicate greens. Osage orange is sold both as wood chips and as a concentrated extract. If you're using wood chips, weigh out as much as you need, cut them in small pieces, then place them in a nylon stocking. Put them in a pot, covered with water, to soak overnight. The next day, bring the water to a boil and simmer one hour, then remove the stocking of chips from the dyebath. If using concentrate, simply measure out the required amount and dissolve it in hot water.

Add the prepared fiber to the Osage orange dyebath, bring to a boil, and simmer for 30 minutes to "set" the yellow color. Then remove the fiber, add the required amount of Saxon blue solution, and stir. Return the fiber to the dyepot and simmer for another 30 minutes.

Using Saxon blue indigo with black walnut—Black walnut hulls normally give a range of brown dyes, but in combination with Saxon blue indigo they can produce rich forest greens, lovely light greens, and all the shades in between. To make the walnut dyebath, weigh the walnuts, put them in a mesh bag, and soak overnight. The next day, bring to a boil and boil, covered, for at least an hour before straining off the dyebath. Add the prepared fiber and simmer for one hour. Depending on the amount of walnuts used, the color can range from pale beige to dark brown. Lift the fiber out of the bath, add the required amount of Saxon blue solution, then return the fiber to the dyepot and simmer for another 30 minutes.

Using Saxon blue indigo with kamala—Unlike the several dye combinations described above, kamala and Saxon blue indigo cannot be used as a mixture. In this recipe, the fiber is first dyed yellow with kamala and then top-dyed in a separate indigo dyebath.

Kamala powder will dissolve only in an alkaline solution. When you first put the measured amount of kamala powder into a dyepot of water, it will appear to be curdling. Adding washing soda makes the water alkaline enough so that the curds dissolve, making a yellow solution. I start with a teaspoonful and add more if needed depending on the initial pH of the water. Stir well. As soon as the kamala powder is dissolved, the dyebath is ready for use. Add the wetted fiber, bring the water to a boil, and simmer for one hour. The fiber will be a beautiful warm yellow when you remove it from the kamala dyebath. Spin it to extract any excess yellow dye.

Add the required amount of Saxon blue solution to a separate dyepot of clean water and enter the fiber. Bring the water to a boil and simmer for 30 minutes.

Using Saxon blue indigo with lichen—A dyer in Oregon gave me a supply of a lichen that forms bushy, branching clusters on dead tree limbs there. It seems to be a species of the genus *Cladonia*. Alone, the lichen gives a bright yellow dye, and it's ideal combined with indigo to make vivid greens.

Weigh out the lichen, add it to a dyepot of water, bring the water to a boil, and simmer for one hour. Strain the dye solution into another pot, add the warmed, wetted fiber, and simmer for 30 minutes to "set" the yellow color. Remove the fiber, add the required amount of Saxon blue solution, and stir. Return the fiber to the dyepot and simmer for another 30 minutes.

INDIGO   For very dark shades of indigo, I would probably use the more traditional method described in the introduction to this section. The Saxon blue method that I've used here is much easier, and produces attractive medium shades as well as working well with other dyestuffs. The actual colors are much greener—tending toward turquoise and teal—than the photographs are able to show.

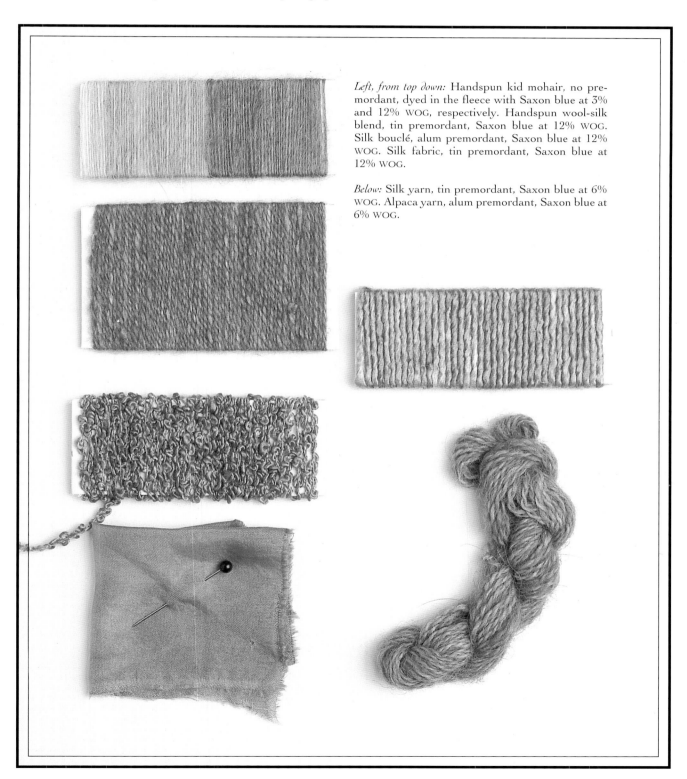

Left, from top down: Handspun kid mohair, no premordant, dyed in the fleece with Saxon blue at 3% and 12% WOG, respectively. Handspun wool-silk blend, tin premordant, Saxon blue at 12% WOG. Silk bouclé, alum premordant, Saxon blue at 12% WOG. Silk fabric, tin premordant, Saxon blue at 12% WOG.

Below: Silk yarn, tin premordant, Saxon blue at 6% WOG. Alpaca yarn, alum premordant, Saxon blue at 6% WOG.

INDIGO & COCHINEAL It takes only a little bit of cochineal to influence Saxon blue in a purple direction. The green cast that characterizes fibers dyed only with Saxon blue are not apparent in these samples.

Above: Brushed mohair, alum premordant, 3% cochineal and 35% and 25% Saxon blue respectively. 3% tartaric acid and 0.25% tin were added to the dyebath. *Below:* Brushed mohair yarn and alpaca yarn, tin premordant, 15% Saxon blue and 5% cochineal, 5% tartaric acid in the dyebath. The different fibers take the color very differently.

Above: Alpaca yarn and wool fabric, alum premordant, 25% Saxon blue and 3% cochineal, 1.5% tartaric acid in the dyebath. Again, the two fibers take the color differently. *Below:* Handspun silk-wool blend. The left sample has no premordant and the right was premordanted with tin. Both samples were dyed with 12% Saxon blue and 5% cochineal with 5% tartaric acid and 0.24% tin in the dyebath.

INDIGO & BLACK WALNUT Dyeing fiber first with black walnuts and then adding Saxon blue to the bath results in rich, earthy shades of green, olive, and blue. Most of the samples on this page use black walnuts at 15% WOG. The percentages of Saxon blue vary, producing the different hues.

Left, from the top down: Handspun wool yarn, no mordant, 10% black walnut and 20% Saxon blue. Alpaca yarn, no mordant, with 15% and 10% black walnut, respectively, and 20% Saxon blue. Wool fabrics, no mordant, all dyed with 15% black walnut and Saxon blue at 30%, 20%, 15%, and 10% respectively.

Below: Brushed mohair, tin premordant, 15% black walnut and 15% and 30% Saxon blue, respectively.

INDIGO & VARIOUS YELLOWS Be sure and read the introduction to this section for details on how to combine indigo with various yellows. These samples are largely the result of using the third or fourth bath of a strong yellow formulation with a very small percentage of Saxon blue.

Brushed mohair, tin pre-mordant, 100% goldenrod, 3% Saxon blue

Alpaca, no mordant, 100% goldenrod, 3% Saxon blue

Silk, alum premordant, 100% marigold, 3% Saxon blue

Alpaca, tin premordant, 100% goldenrod, 3% Saxon blue

Mohair, alum premordant, 100% goldenrod, 3% Saxon blue, ammonia afterbath

Silk-wool blend, alum premordant, 50% Osage orange, 6% Saxon blue

Silk, tin premordant, 50% Osage orange, 6% Saxon blue

Brushed mohair, tin premordant, 100% Oregon lichen, 3% Saxon blue

Brushed mohair, tin premordant, 100% goldenrod, 3% Saxon blue, ammonia afterbath

Alpaca, alum premordant, 50% goldenrod, 3% Saxon blue, copper "greening" afterbath

Silk-wool blend, tin premordant, 6% Saxon blue overdyed with 15% kamala

Loop mohair, tin premordant, 50% Oregon lichen, 1.5% Saxon blue

SELECTED BIBLIOGRAPHY

Adrosko, Rita J. *Natural Dyes and Home Dyeing*. New York: Dover, 1971.

Buchanan, Rita. *A Weaver's Garden*. Loveland, Colorado: Interweave Press, 1987.

Coon, Nelson. *The Dictionary of Useful Plants*. Emmaus, Pennsylvania: Rodale Press, 1974.

Cox, Jeff and Marilyn. *The Perennial Garden*. Emmaus, Pennsylvania: Rodale Press, 1985.

Erichsen-Brown, Charlotte. *Use of Plants for the Past 500 Years*. Breezy Creeks Press, 1979.

Krochmal, Arnold and Connie. *The Complete Illustrated Book of Dyes from Natural Sources*. Garden City, New York: Doubleday, 1974.

Lima, Patrick. *Perennial Garden*. Altona, Manitoba: D. W. Friesen & Sons, 1987.

McGrath, Judy Waldner. *Dyes from Lichens & Plants*. Toronto, Ontario: Van Nostrand Reinhold, 1977.

Miller, Dorothy. *Indigo, From Seed to Dye*. Aptos, California: Indigo Press, 1984.

Mulligan, Gerald A. *Common Weeds of Canada*. Toronto, Ontario: New Canada Publications, 1987.

Novah, F. A. *The Pictorial Encyclopedia of Plants and Flowers*. London: Hamlyn Publishing Group, 1966.

Schetky, Ethel Jane McD. *Handbook on Dye Plants and Dyeing*. Brooklyn, New York: Brooklyn Botanic Garden, 1982.

Van de Vrande, Iet. *Groot Plantaardig Verfboek*. Amsterdam: Cantecleer, 1979.

Weigle, Palmy. *Natural Plant Dyeing*. Brooklyn, New York: Brooklyn Botanic Garden, 1978.

SELECTED SOURCES

Most weaving and spinning shops carry some natural dyestuffs and mordants. Be sure to check with your local sources, as well as with local pharmacies for mordants. The following suppliers have mail order offerings.

Aurora Silk, 5806 North Vancouver Avenue, Portland, OR 97217. Price list free.

Creek Water Wool Works, PO Box 716, Salem, OR 97308. Catalog $3.00.

Dharma Trading Company, PO Box 150916, San Rafael, CA 94915. Catalog free.

Earth Guild, 33 Hayward Street, Asheville, NC 28801. Catalog free.

Louët Sales, Box 267, Ogdensburg, NY 13669 or RR4, Prescott, Ontario. Catalog $2.00.

The Mannings, PO Box 687, East Berlin, PA 17316. Catalog $1.50.

Rio Grande Weaver's Supply. 216-B Paseo del Pueblo Norte, Taos, NM 87571. Catalog $1.00.

The Weaver's Knot, 121 Cleveland Street, Greenville, SC 29601. Catalog $3.00.

The Woolery, RD 1, Genoa, NY 13071. Catalog $2.00.

I N D E X